· THOU ART THAT ·

JOSEPH CAMPBELL

· THOU ART THAT ·

TRANSFORMING RELIGIOUS METAPHOR

Edited and with a foreword by Eugene Kennedy, Ph.D.

 JOSEPH CAMPBELL FOUNDATION

 NEW WORLD LIBRARY
NOVATO, CALIFORNIA

New World Library
14 Pamaron Way
Novato, California 94949
www.newworldlibrary.com
(800) 972-6657

Cover design: Laura Beers
Type design: Tona Pearce Myers

Library of Congress Cataloging-in-Publication Data

Campbell, Joseph, 1904–1987
Thou art that : transforming religious metaphor / Joseph Campbell ; edited with an
    introduction by Eugene Kennedy.
      p.   cm. — (The collected works of Joseph Campbell)
Includes bibliographical references and index.
    ISBN 1-57731-202-3 (perfect : alk. paper)
    1. Metaphor—Religious aspects—Christianity. I. Kennedy, Eugene C. II. Title.
BR115.L25 C36 2001
    230—dc21   2001002531

First printing, October 2001
ISBN 1-57731-202-3
Printed in Canada on acid-free, recycled paper
Distributed to the trade by Publishers Group West

10 9

For
Jean Erdman Campbell

CONTENTS

ABOUT THE COLLECTED WORKS OF JOSEPH CAMPBELL   ix
EDITOR'S FOREWORD BY EUGENE KENNEDY   xi

CHAPTER I

METAPHOR AND RELIGIOUS MYSTERY   1

The Meaning of Myth   1
What Myths Do   2
Metaphor, the Native Tongue of Myth   6
Metaphor and Mystery   8

CHAPTER II

THE EXPERIENCE OF RELIGIOUS MYSTERY   11

Symbolism and Religious Experience   11
Experiencing Mystery   12

CHAPTER III

OUR NOTIONS OF GOD   17

Elements of Our Experience of the Mystery of God   24
Symbols: Out of Time and Place   28

CHAPTER IV

THE RELIGIOUS IMAGINATION
AND THE RULES OF TRADITIONAL THEOLOGY   33

Imagination and Its Relation to Theological Inquiry   37

CHAPTER V

SYMBOLS OF THE JUDEO-CHRISTIAN TRADITION   43

What Kinds of Gods Have We?   43
Genesis   49
Abraham, Father of the Jewish People   53

CHAPTER VI

UNDERSTANDING THE SYMBOLS OF
JUDEO-CHRISTIAN SPIRITUALITY   61

The Virgin Birth   62
The Cave   65
The Infant   66
Flight into Egypt   68
The Child as Teacher   68
The Messiah   70
Miracles   72
The Last Supper   73
Judas   75
Crucifixion   76
The Cross   76
The End of the World   83

CHAPTER VII

QUESTION PERIOD   85

APPENDIX

A DISCUSSION   101
Introductory Note   101
Earthrise—The Dawning of a New Spiritual Awareness   102

CHAPTER NOTES   115
A JOSEPH CAMPBELL BIBLIOGRAPHY   121
INDEX   125
ABOUT THE AUTHOR   133
ABOUT THE JOSEPH CAMPBELL FOUNDATION   135

ABOUT THE COLLECTED WORKS OF
JOSEPH CAMPBELL

At his death in 1987, Joseph Campbell left a significant body of published work that explored his lifelong passion, the complex of universal myths and symbols that he called "Mankind's one great story." He also left, however, a large volume of unreleased work: uncollected articles, notes, letters, and diaries, as well as audio- and videotape recorded lectures.

The Joseph Campbell Foundation was founded in 1991 to preserve, protect, and perpetuate Campbell's work. The Foundation has undertaken to archive his papers and recordings in digital format, and to publish previously unavailable material and out-of-print works as *The Collected Works of Joseph Campbell.*

THE COLLECTED WORKS OF JOSEPH CAMPBELL
Robert Walter, Executive Editor
David Kudler, Managing Editor

EDITOR'S FOREWORD

"Tat tvam asi" is a phrase that appears often in these collected spiritual reflections of the late Joseph Campbell. These words also inscribe a signature of celebration on his life and work. Translated from the Sanskrit as "thou art that," this epigram captures Campbell's generous spirit just as it does his scholarly focus. The great student of mythology not only understood the profound spiritual implications of the phrase but, quite unselfconsciously, lived by them as well.

Joseph Campbell was fond of asking Schopenhauer's question, found in his essay *On the Foundations of Morality:* "How is it possible that suffering that is neither my own nor of my concern should immediately affect me as though it were my own, and with such force that it moves me to action?... This is something really mysterious, something for which Reason can provide no explanation, and for which no basis can be found in practical experience. It is not unknown even to the most hard-hearted and self-interested. Examples appear every day before our eyes of instant responses of the kind, without reflection, one person helping another, coming to his aid, even setting his own life in clear danger for someone whom he has seen for the first time, having nothing more in mind than that the other is in need and in peril of his life...." [1]

Schopenhauer's response, one Campbell delighted in making his own, was that the immediate reaction and response represented the breakthrough of a metaphysical realization best rendered as "thou art that."[2] This presupposes, as the German philosopher wrote, his identification with someone not himself, a penetration of the barrier between persons so that the other was no longer perceived as an indifferent stranger but as a person "in whom I suffer, in spite of the fact that his skin does not enfold my nerves."[3]

This fundamental insight, as Schopenhauer continued, reveals that "my own true inner being actually exists in every living creature... [and] is the ground of that compassion *(Mitleid)* upon which all true, that is to say, unselfish, virtue rests and whose expression is in every good deed."[4]

Joseph Campbell was not only moved by compassion in his personal relationships, as anybody who ever heard him speak or reads his works can easily sense, but he also grasped that this spiritual realization was central to understanding the metaphorical language through which both mythology and religion, whose images and energy flow from a common source in human imagination, express themselves. "The metaphors of any mythology," as he wrote, "may be defined as affect signs derived from intuitions of just this play of the Self through all the forms of a local manner of life, made manifest through ritualized representations, pedagogical narratives, prayers, meditations, annual festivals, and the like, in such a way that all members of the relevant community may be held, both in mind and in sentiment, to its knowledge and thus moved to live in accord."[5]

For Campbell, mythology was, in a sense, the powerful cathedral organ through which the tonal resonations of a hundred separate pipes were fused into the same extraordinary music. What was common in these multiplied themes was their human origin, as if each were a vessel of the same eternal cry of the spirit, inflected in extraordinary and dazzling variations, in the field of time. We men and women find ourselves in the creative expressions of our human longings, aspirations, and tragedies of our own particular tradition. Indeed, so familiar and almost natural do these seem to us that they almost exclude the possibility that the same feelings and ideals might be expressed quite differently through some other tradition. If we listen and look carefully, however, we discover ourselves in the literature, rites, and symbols of others, even though at first they seem distorted and alien to us. Thou art that, Campbell would judge, citing the underlying spiritual intuition of his life and work, *tat tvam asi.*

What Campbell heard, in these varied and sometimes all but indecipherable choruses, was a shared sense of wonder and awe at the mystery of being. The compassion that Campbell recognized as the most ennobling of all human reactions was not, as he well understood, evoked by all traditions with the same concern or conviction. The Judeo-Christian tradition, however, out of which he himself came, was a powerful source of teaching about compassion in a way that was not as sensitively developed or emphasized in the customs of some other cultures. When the Judeo-Christian tradition was brought to lands where it had not been known, it brought its often-criticized defects and excesses. It also brought, however, something new and revolutionary, a well-developed sense of compassion for the suffering of others.

That is why, in gathering together, indeed, in some cases, in grafting onto one branch, Joseph Campbell's many reflections on the Judeo-Christian spiritual heritage, the theme of compassion emerges so eloquently. Many who were close to Joseph Campbell share a conviction about this remarkable, self-directed student of comparative religion. So absorbed was he when conversing about his subject that he was hardly aware of himself or of how much he knew. At times, questions from an audience or friends would elicit remarkable observations or explanations. These resembled the mythological treasures in the field, of which he sometimes spoke, that could only be unearthed by accident. "Where you stumble and fall," he would say, recalling a theme about our common humanity, "there you discover the gold."

This applies to the journey that the making of this book required, for many of Joseph Campbell's insights into Judeo-Christian symbols and myths were embedded in lectures in which they were but examples of broader themes. So, too, question periods mined out of him, so to speak, treasures of learning that might not otherwise have come to the surface. These replies, which sometimes expanded into miniature lectures, often illuminated vast landscapes of Biblical history. They were delivered, however, in a way that placed the questioners on an equal plane with him, as if they were looking at the same problem together from the same equal fund of knowledge about the Bible, religion, and mythology. Many of these have been worked into the texts of this volume so that, perhaps for the first time in one place, much of what Joseph Campbell knew about the origins, symbols, and meanings of Judeo-Christian spirituality are presented together.

This is, of course, not a new way to produce a cohesive book. It is the method of mythology itself just as it is of many of the collected sayings and writings of any religious tradition. Some of these chapters are editions of specific lectures, as mentioned in the note of explanation. More typically, they represent the integration of several versions of the same lecture, to insure the best evocation of the speaker's style and insights. Joseph Campbell the lecturer is, as previously observed, different from Joseph Campbell the polished prose-stylist. This allows us to encounter the speaker who engaged his hearers as a master teacher does his students and, like the historian Herodotus, knows how to use digressions as part of his plan.

Joseph Campbell, like an archaeologist calling back to life an ancient village known only by its dried up bones and artifacts, reveals the vitality in what seem, even to many Jews and Christians, dead and brittle relics of belief. He evokes, for example, the living quality of the Jewish people and the symbolic richness of the Old Testament, which by the reverse alchemy of those who regard them with stifling Cecil B. DeMille literalness, has been spiritually devalued over the centuries. Nothing will better belie the false accusation made after his death, of Campbell being anti-Semitic, than the unfeigned sensitivity and respect with which he illuminates the majesty of Jewish belief and history.

In the same way, Joseph Campbell reacquaints Christians with the aura of meanings that hover about the religious incidents and stories of the New Testament. As in treating Jewish history, it is in this aura—that is, in the connotations that by their nature blossom out of metaphors—that the deepest significance of the stories of Jesus' life and work are to be found. To describe the testaments as myth is not, as Campbell points out, to debunk them. The contemporary impression of myth as falsehood has, as Campbell illustrates in these pages by recalling an obnoxious and ill-informed interviewer, led people to think of them as fantasies passing as truth. But mythology is a vessel of the truth that is far more reliable than census and almanac figures, which, subject to time as myth is not, are out of date as soon as they are printed. Joseph Campbell's purpose in exploring the biblical myths is not to dismiss them as unbelievable but to lay open once again their living and nourishing core.

Many elements of the Bible seem lifeless and unbelievable because they have been regarded as historical facts instead of metaphorical representations of spiritual realities. They have been applied in a concrete way to great figures, such as Moses and John the Baptist, as if they were real-time accounts of their actions. That this heavy emphasis on the historical rather than the spiritual should have continued into the twenty-first century illustrates the lag-time that the leaders of institutional religions have allowed to open up between their static ideas and the rapidly developing understandings of solid new scholarship. A failure to follow Pope John XXIII's injunction to "read the signs of the times" leaves them behind even their own times.

There is little evident progress in formal religious teaching—it fails to incorporate or even to acknowledge the advances in research that allow us to read with renewed understanding the great documents and traditions of the dominant Western religions. The spiritual needs of people are neglected by religious leaders who insist on reasserting the historical-factual character of religious metaphors, thereby distorting and debasing their meaning.

This leaves organized religion to work through, in a contemporary version of Purgatory, an endless summer of "monkey trials," such as the celebrated 1925 Scopes trial in Dayton, Tennessee, in which William Jennings Bryan's well-motivated testimony to the literal, historical interpretation of the Bible was destroyed under cross-examination by Clarence Darrow. This encounter, itself mythologized in a play and film, has perpetuated the tragically mistaken idea that science and religion are opposed and mutually exclusive avenues to the truth of our lives and universe. The drama of the trial, its details rearranged for dramatic purposes, contains a truth that existed before and lives on after the case itself: the tragic consequences that follow when, for the best of intentions and the worst of reasons, men battle against truth to defend their outdated beliefs. Thus institutional religious leaders unnecessarily embrace a frail caricature of religion which is easily demolished by popular lecturers, totally out of their depths in theology, such as the late astronomer Carl Sagan.

Failure to appreciate the metaphorical nature of religious literature and discourse has led to numerous embarrassing crusades or expeditions to defend the biblical accounts of creation. Bitter fights over "creationist" versus "evolutionary" theories in textbooks are but one example of why the Scopes trial has become mythologized. Men mount expensive expeditions to locate the remains of Noah's ark on Mt. Ararat but, of course, they never find it. They believe, however, that they have just missed it for the ark must literally have existed and its timbers must rest somewhere, still hidden from their eyes. The ark, however, can be found easily and without travel by those who understand that it is a mythological vessel in an extraordinary story whose point is not historical documentation but spiritual enlightenment. To appreciate Genesis as myth is not to destroy that book but to discover again its spiritual vitality and relevance.

This stuttering inability to catch up with the mythological structures of the religious imagination has isolated fundamentalist believers in their fierce and often violent defenses of literalist, concrete beliefs in every section of the world. The Scopes trial ended in the unfortunate shaming of an otherwise great man, William Jennings Bryan, and the demeaning of religion as a hodgepodge of beliefs and superstitions that were no longer relevant to the twentieth century. Such outcomes were bad enough. They are mild, however, compared to the results of the wars that continue to be waged to vindicate concrete interpretations of religious teachings.

In the selections that compose this volume, Joseph Campbell provides a new but not novel basis for our understanding of the Judeo-Christian tradition. He is preoccupied with solving the enormous problems that flow from institutional religion's ongoing misinterpretation of spiritual metaphors as historical facts. Metaphor comes from the Greek *meta,* a passing over, or a going from one place to another, and *phorein,* to move or to carry. Metaphors carry us from one place to another, they enable us to cross boundaries that would otherwise be closed to us. Spiritual truths that transcend time and space can only be borne in metaphorical vessels whose meaning is found in their connotations—that is, in the cloud of witnesses to the many sides of truth that they spontaneously evoke—not in their denotations, the hard, factual, unidimensional casings of their historical reference.

Thus, the Virgin Birth, as the reader will learn, does not refer to the biological condition of Mary, the mother of Jesus, but to a rebirth of the spirit that everyone can experience. The Promised Land refers not to a geographical location but to the territory of the human heart which anyone can enter. Yet sheaves of condemnations have been issued and never-ending wars have been fought over basic misapplications of these very metaphors, which should enable us to cross the boundaries of time and space, rather than to remain frustrated and forever in place on the dusty stage set of their concrete historical period. Denotations are singular, time bound, and nonspiritual; the connotations of religious metaphor are rich, timeless, and refer not to somebody else in the outer world of another era but to us and our inner spiritual experience right now.

Joseph Campbell also sketches the mythic religious theme that explains the hesitant character of the leaders of institutional religions. Christ, as the reader will recall or rediscover in this book, chose Peter, saying, in effect, "You do not understand spiritual things, therefore, I will make you head of my church." So, too, the Buddha chose the cumbersome Ananda for a similar role. Perhaps, as Campbell repeatedly observes, the spiritual quest cannot be undertaken other than by ourselves—that is, we cannot expect bishops and rabbis to make it for us. Thus, in the story of the Arthurian knights, each was to set out in search of the Grail, a spiritual rather than a material goal, by "entering the forest at its darkest part," that is, at the place where no one has cut a path before. The inertia of organized religion is a constant challenge to spiritual growth: inevitably we must make our own path rather than follow someone else's.

Joseph Campbell's own religious heritage was Roman Catholic. He formally abandoned the Church when, as a student of mythology, he felt that the Church was teaching a literal and concrete faith that could not sustain an adult. By the age of twenty-five, Campbell like others of his time had moved out of the structures of Catholicism. Campbell later softened what at one point seemed to be bitter feelings toward Catholicism, acknowledging the pedagogical need to teach children through concrete interpretations, rather than through metaphors they could not understand. He never, however, returned to attending Mass, although he understood and profoundly underscored its potent symbolism in many of his lectures.

No true believers of any tradition will find their faith diminished by reading Joseph Campbell. They will rather feel that they need not surrender their traditions in order to see more deeply into their most sacred teachings and rituals.

At the end of his life, according to Pythia Peay in an article on "Campbell and Catholicism," "Campbell was undergoing laser treatment at St. Francis Hospital in Honolulu. His room, like every other room in that hospital, had a small brass crucifix hanging on the wall. Instead of the usual suffering Christ with head bowed and body bloodied, the figure on the cross in Campbell's room was fully clothed, with head erect, eyes open, and arms outstretched in what seemed an almost joyful embrace of the divine." This was the Triumphant Christ of whom Campbell had often written as a symbol of the zeal of eternity for incarnation in time, which involves the breaking up of the one into the many and the acceptance of the sufferings in a confident and joyful manner.

According to Peay, Campbell "experienced profoundly the depths of the Christian symbol" during what were the last weeks of his life. She quotes his wife Jean Erdman as saying, "He was thrilled to see that, because for him this was the mystical meaning of Christ that reflected the state of at-one-ment with the Father." In the hospital room, according to his wife, "he experienced emotionally what he had before understood intellectually. Seeing this image in a Catholic hospital room helped release him from the conflict that he had had with his childhood religion." [6]

Joseph Campbell was fully incarnated in time, a lively and charming man, brimming with enthusiasm for the great mystery of being in which he was himself fully invested. But he had to embrace death before his message was delivered to the enormous audience that first became acquainted with him through the Bill Moyers television interviews. He experienced a resurrection to which, in one measure or another, we are all witnesses. Cruelly, he was then to undergo a crucifixion at the hands of critics, some of whom fulfilled the Judas role by betraying the help and models he had given them to aid their own studies of mythology. Others seemed to envy his sudden fame and to be infuriated that he had achieved, in a way from beyond eternity, something that had been denied to them on their worn treadmill of time.

Still others prefer to misread, misinterpret, or take somebody else's word for what Campbell has written. We may take, for our example, the Catholic theologian who claims that Campbell described the Catholic Mass as nothing more than a Julia Child show. What Campbell actually suggested, as readers will discover in these pages, was that the richness of the mystery had been stripped out of the Mass by reformers who translated it into the vernacular and turned the priest toward the people. It was, in his apt comparison, the reformers who did not understand symbols who had made the Mass more like a television show than a sacramental meal.

Joseph Campbell needs no defenders against such critics. He would have been as surprised and dismayed by them as he would have at his great fame. His works will, because of their inherent character, survive the critics as well. Indeed, in Campbell's many books and talks we find the vocabulary that we will need to speak spiritually in the century in whose shadow we now live. This book is an effort to provide the first draft of a lexicon that allows people to penetrate and breathe the spirit into the sails of the great vessel of the Judeo-Christian institutions that now seem becalmed.

As this is written, the Carter Center for Peace Studies in Atlanta is monitoring a total of one hundred and twelve conflicts, many of them based on conflicting ethnic claims, throughout the world. They threaten to shatter the concept of a unified world and to return millions of people to embittered and embattled isolation from one another. Joseph Campbell's central message is that these ethnic divisions are the bitter harvest of the distortions of religious teachings planted long ago. When spiritual rights are demanded on the basis of religious metaphors as facts and geography instead of as symbols of the heart and spirit, a bitterly divided world arises with the inevitability of great tragedy.

Even the word compassion has been devalued in our day into a protoplasmic concept that is as ungrounded in sacrifice as it is soaked in undifferentiated sentimentality. It has been absorbed, as a small democracy is incorporated into a totalitarian neighbor, by the New Age enthusiasts who have coated it in astral vagueness. Compassion, however, demands much more of our character, requiring that we each make a hero's journey into the far reaches of the lives of people that seem different from us. This is fundamentally a spiritual experience and we need not leave home, not even the chair we are sitting on, to join ourselves to it.

The exercise of compassion, identified as the highest religious and spiritual ideal in Joseph Campbell's work, requires a triumph over the ancient obstacles that arise with flaming swords before every generation: Desire and Fear of Death. Campbell's labors may be compared to those of a master art restorer who wants us to see again the masterpiece of our Western spiritual heritage as it was before it was so darkened and changed by history.

Its sweeping canvas has been painted over many times during the centuries, sometimes by its enemies, too often by its friends, so that the vibrancy of the original images and colors have been lost. Campbell's labor, like that which uncovered vivid colors beneath the glaucoma-like dullness that had obscured Michelangelo's Sistine Chapel, allows us to see once more, as the blind did in the Gospel, the brilliance of creation.

In a true sense, we might say that Joseph Campbell preaches the End of the World, that great metaphor of spirituality that has been so explosively employed by those who have taken its denotative skin and thrown aside its connotative meat. For, as Campbell explains, the End of the World is not a cataclysmic event to whose final judgmental terror we draw ever closer. The End of the World comes every day for those whose spiritual insight allows them to see the world as it is, transparent to transcendence, a sacrament of mystery, or, as the poet William Blake wrote, "infinite." The End of the World is, therefore, metaphoric of our spiritual beginning rather than our harsh and fiery ending.

The Judeo-Christian spiritual tradition, restored by Joseph Campbell, is quite different from the splintered and self-righteous religious sectarianism that sets people against each other in warfare that is as unforgiving as it is unending. The tradition's most significant teaching is indeed that of compassion, which requires that we die to ourselves in order to rise to that vision that reveals that we share the same human nature with all other persons. *Tat tvam asi.*

Joseph Campbell's message for the twenty-first century is not apocalyptic. It is hopeful, because it roots us once more in the foundations of the

Judeo-Christian tradition, and in the task of conquering the desire and fear that alone exile us from that garden in which, far from viewing each other in shame, we embrace the humanity with which we are all signed.

Tat tvam asi. Thou art that.

Eugene Kennedy, Ph.D.

CHAPTER I

METAPHOR AND RELIGIOUS MYSTERY

THE MEANING OF MYTH

Let me begin by explaining the history of my impulse to place metaphor at the center of our exploration of Western spirituality.

When the first volume of my *Historical Atlas of World Mythology, The Way of the Animal Powers*7 came out, the publishers sent me on a publicity tour. This is the worst kind of all possible tours because you move unwillingly to those disc jockeys and newspaper people, themselves unwilling to read the book they are supposed to talk to you about, in order to give it public visibility.

The first question I would be asked was always, "What is a myth?" That is a fine beginning for an intelligent conversation. In one city, however, I walked into a broadcasting station for a live half-hour program where the interviewer was a young, smart-looking man who immediately warned me, "I'm tough, I put it right to you. I've studied law."

The red light went on and he began argumentatively, "The word 'myth,' means 'a lie.' Myth is a lie."

So I replied with my definition of myth. "No, myth is not a lie. A whole mythology is an organization of symbolic images and narratives, metaphorical of the possibilities of human experience and the fulfillment of a given culture at a given time."

"It's a lie," he countered.

"It's a metaphor."

"It's a lie."

This went on for about twenty minutes. Around four or five minutes before the end of the program, I realized that this interviewer did not really know what a metaphor was. I decided to treat him as he was treating me.

"No," I said, "I tell you it's metaphorical. You give me an example of a metaphor."

He replied, "You give me an example."

I resisted, "No, I'm asking the question this time." I had not taught school for thirty years for nothing. "And I want you to give me an example of a metaphor."

The interviewer was utterly baffled and even went so far as to say, "Let's get in touch with some school teacher." Finally, with something like a minute and a half to go, he rose to the occasion and said, "I'll try. My friend John runs very fast. People say he runs like a deer. There's a metaphor."

As the last seconds of the interview ticked off, I replied, "That is not the metaphor. The metaphor is: John *is* a deer."

He shot back, "That's a lie."

"No," I said, "That is a metaphor."

And the show ended. What does that incident suggest about our common understanding of metaphor?

It made me reflect that half the people in the world think that the metaphors of their religious traditions, for example, are facts. And the other half contends that they are not facts at all. As a result we have people who consider themselves believers because they accept metaphors as facts, and we have others who classify themselves as atheists because they think religious metaphors are lies.

What Myths Do

I view traditional mythologies as serving four functions. The first function is that of reconciling consciousness to the preconditions of its own existence—that is, of aligning waking consciousness to the *mysterium tremendum* of this universe, *as it is.*

The primitive mythologies—including most of the archaic mythologies—are concerned with helping people to assent or say yes to that. They do it, however, in the most monstrous way, by enacting rituals of horrendous murder right in front of onlookers' eyes with the whole community participating in it. If one cannot affirm that, one is not affirming life, for that is what life is. There came then in human history a moment when consciousness refused to accept this interpretation and there arose a system of mythologies concerned with helping people to remove themselves, to place themselves at a distance from this conception of basic experience.

The Zoroastrian religion appeared, presenting the notion that the world was originally good—harmless, so to say—and that an evil principle moved in to precipitate a fall. Out of that fall came this unfortunate, unhappy, unintended situation known as the human condition. By following the doctrine of Zoroaster, by participating in a good work, persons associate themselves with the forces of restoration, eliminating the infection of evil and moving on toward the good again.

Essentially, this is the mythology, in broad terms, found in the biblical tradition: the idea of a good creation and a subsequent fall. Instead of blaming the fall on an evil principle antecedent to man, the biblical tradition blamed it on man himself. The work of redemption restores the good situation and, this completed, will bring about the end of the world as we know it—that is, the world of conflict and contest, that universe of life eating life.

Whether one thinks of the mythology in terms of the affirmation of the world as it is, the negation of the world as it is, or the restoration of the world to what it ought to be, the first function of mythology is to arouse in the mind a sense of awe before this situation through one of three ways of participating in it: by moving out, moving in, or effecting a correction.

This I would regard as the essentially religious function of mythology—that is, the mystical function, which represents the discovery and recognition of the dimension of the mystery of being.

The second function of a traditional mythology is interpretive, to present a consistent image of the order of the cosmos. At about 3200 B.C. the concept of a cosmic order came into being, along with the notion that society and men and women should participate in that cosmic order because it is, in fact, the basic order of one's life.

Earlier than this, in primitive societies, the focus of awe was not on a cosmic order but on the extraordinary appearance of the animal that acts differently from others of its species, or on a certain species of animal that seems to be particularly clever and bright, or on some striking aspect of the landscape. Such exceptional things predominate in the primitive world mythologies. In the period of the high civilizations, however, one comes to the experience of a great mysterious *tremendum* that manifests itself so impersonally that one cannot even pray to it, one can only be in awe of it. The gods themselves are simply agents of that great high mystery, the secret of which is found in mathematics. This can still be observed in our sciences, in which the mathematics of time and space are regarded as the veil through which the great mystery, the *tremendum,* shows itself.

The science, in all of the traditional mythologies, reflected that of its time. It is not surprising that the Bible reflects the cosmology of the third millennium B.C. Those who do not understand the metaphor, the language of religious revelation, find themselves up against the images that they accept or contest as facts.

One of the most stunning experiences of this century occurred in 1968 on a great venture around the moon. On Christmas Eve, the first verses of Genesis were read by astronauts, three men flying around the moon. The incongruity was that they were several thousand miles beyond the highest heaven conceived of at the time when the Book of Genesis was written, when such science as there was held the concept of a flat earth. There they were, in one moment remarking on how dry the moon was, and in the next, reading of how the waters above and the waters beneath had been walled off.

One of the most marvelous moments of that contemporary experience was described in stately imagery that just did not fit. The moment deserved a more appropriate religious text. Yet it came to us with all the awe of something wise, something resonant of our origins, even though it really was not. The old metaphors were taken as factual accounts of creation. Modern cosmology had left that whole little kindergarten image of the universe far, far behind, but, as an illustration of popular misconception, the metaphors of the Bible, which were not intended as fact, were spoken by men who believed that they were to millions who also believed that these metaphors were factual.

The third function of a traditional mythology is to validate and support a specific moral order, that order of the society out of which that mythology arose. All mythologies come to us in the field of a certain specific culture and must speak to us through the language and symbols of that culture. In traditional mythologies, the notion is really that the moral order is organically related to or somehow of a piece with the cosmic order.

Through this third function, mythology reinforces the moral order by shaping the person to the demands of a specific geographically and historically conditioned social group.

As an example, the primitive rites of initiation, which treated people quite harshly, were intended to solve the problem of getting growing persons over the first great threshold of their development. These rites, commonly, included scarification and certain minor surgeries. Such rites were carried out so that persons could realize that they no longer had the same body they had as children. They could look at themselves afterwards and see that they were different, that they were no longer children. This socially ordered cutting, branding, and cropping was to incorporate them, mind and body, into a larger, more enduring cultural body whose explanatory mythology became their own. The force here, it must be observed, is found in society rather than in nature.

Thus it was the social authority in India, for example, which maintained the caste system as well as the rituals and mythology of suttee. It is precisely here, we might note, that a great difficulty arises. A real danger exists when social institutions press on people mythological structures that no longer match their human experience. For example, when certain religious or political interpretations of human life are insisted upon, mythic dissociation can occur. Through mythic dissociation, persons reject or are cut off from effective explanatory notions about the order of their lives.

The fourth function of traditional mythology is to carry the individual through the various stages and crises of life—that is, to help persons grasp the unfolding of life with integrity. This wholeness means that individuals will experience significant events, from birth through midlife to death, as in accord with, first, themselves, and, secondly, with their culture, as well as, thirdly, the universe, and, lastly, with that *mysterium tremendum* beyond themselves and all things.

Metaphor, the Native Tongue of Myth

The life of a mythology springs from and depends on the metaphoric vigor of its symbols. These deliver more than just an intellectual concept, for such is their inner character that they provide a sense of actual participation in a realization of transcendence. The symbol, energized by metaphor, conveys, not just an idea of the infinite but some realization of the infinite. We must remember, however, that the metaphors of one historically conditioned period, and the symbols they innervate, may not speak to the persons who are living long after that historical moment and whose consciousness has been formed through altogether different experiences.

While times and conditions change drastically, the subject of historical conditioning throughout the centuries, that is the complex psychosomatic unity we call the human person, remains a constant. What Adolph Bastian described as "elementary ideas," and Jung referred to as "archetypes of the collective unconscious" are the biologically rooted motivating powers and connoted references for the mythologies that, cast in the metaphors of changing historical and cultural periods, remain themselves constant.

The metaphors perform their function of speaking to these deep levels of human beings when they arise freshly from the contemporary context of experience. And a new mythology is rapidly becoming a necessity both socially and spiritually as the metaphors of the past, such as the Virgin Birth and the Promised Land, misread consequently as facts, lose their vitality and become concretized. But that new mythology is already implicit among us, native to the mind waiting as the sleeping prince does for the kiss of his beloved, to be awakened by new metaphoric symbolization. These will be derived necessarily from contemporary life, thought, and experience and, as the special language that can of its own power touch the innermost layers of consciousness, provide a reinvigorated mythology to us.

Artists share the calling, according to their disciplines and crafts, to cast the new images of mythology. That is, they provide the contemporary metaphors that allow us to realize the transcendent, infinite, and abundant nature of being as it is. Their metaphors are the essential elements of the symbols that make manifest the radiance of the world just as it is, rather than arguing that it should be one way or the other. They reveal it as it is.

A mythology may be understood as an organization of metaphorical figures connotative of states of mind that are not finally of this or that lo-cation or historical period, even though the figures themselves seem on their surface to suggest such a concrete localization. The metaphorical lan-guages of both mythology and metaphysics are not denotative of actual worlds or gods, but rather connote levels and entities within the person touched by them. Metaphors only seem to describe the outer world of time and place. Their real universe is the spiritual realm of the inner life. The Kingdom of God is within you.

The problem, as we have noted many times, is that these metaphors, which concern that which cannot in any other way be told, are misread prosaically as referring to tangible facts and historical occurrences. The de-notation—that is, the reference in time and space: a particular Virgin Birth, the End of the World—is taken as the message, and the connotation, the rich aura of the metaphor in which its spiritual significance may be de-tected, is ignored altogether. The result is that we are left with the particu-lar "ethnic" inflection of the metaphor, the historical vesture, rather than the living spiritual core.

Inevitably, therefore, the popular understanding is focused on the ritu-als and legends of the local system, and the sense of the symbols is reduced to the concrete goals of a particular political system of socialization. When the language of metaphor is misunderstood and its surface structures be-come brittle, it evokes merely the current time-and-place-bound order of things and its spiritual signal, if transmitted at all, becomes ever fainter.

It has puzzled me greatly that the emphasis in the professional exegesis of the entire Judeo-Christian-Islamic mythology has been on the denota-tive rather than on the connotative meaning of the metaphoric imagery that is its active language. The Virgin Birth, as I have mentioned, has been presented as an historical fact, fashioned into a concrete article of faith over which theologians have argued for hundreds of years, often with grave and disruptive consequences. Practically every mythology in the world has used this "elementary" or co-natural idea of a virgin birth to refer to a spiritual rather than an historical reality. The same, as I have suggested, is true of the metaphor of the Promised Land, which in its denotation plots nothing but a piece of earthly geography to be taken by force. Its connotation—that is, its real meaning—however, is of a spiritual place in the heart that can only be entered by contemplation.

There can be no real progress in understanding how myths function until we understand and allow metaphoric symbols to address, in their own unmodified way, the inner levels of our consciousness. The continuing confusion about the nature and function of metaphor is one of the major obstacles—often placed in our path by organized religions that focus shortsightedly on concrete times and places—to our capacity to experience mystery.

Metaphor and Mystery

Mythology may, in a real sense, be defined as other people's religion. And religion may, in a sense, be understood as a popular misunderstanding of mythology.

Mythology is a system of images that endows the mind and the sentiments with a sense of participation in a field of meaning. The different mythologies define the possible meanings of a person's experience in terms of the knowledge of the historical period, as well as the psychological impact of this knowledge diffused through sociological structures on the complex and psychosomatic system known as the human being.

In a traditional mythology or, if you like, traditional religious system, the imagery and the rituals through which that imagery is integrated into a person's life are presented authoritatively through parents or religious evangelization and the individual is expected to experience the meanings and the sentiments intended.

If, as has happened in the contemporary world, all of the backgrounds of the images of our religious heritage have been transformed, as occurs when we find ourselves in a world of machines rather than in a world of pastoral life, these changed images really cannot and do not communicate the feelings, the sentiments, and the meanings that they did to the people in the world in which these images were developed.

A system of mythological symbols only works if it operates in the field of a community of people who have essentially analogous experiences, or to put it another way, if they share the same realm of life experience.

How, in the contemporary period, can we evoke the imagery that communicates the most profound and most richly developed sense of experiencing life? These images must point past themselves to that ultimate truth which must be told: that life does not have any one absolutely fixed meaning. These images must point past all meanings given, beyond all definitions and relationships, to that really ineffable mystery that is just the existence, the being of ourselves and of our world. If we give that mystery an exact meaning we diminish the experience of its real depth. But when a poet carries the mind into a context of meanings and then pitches it past those, one knows that marvelous rapture that comes from going past all categories of definition. Here we sense the function of metaphor that allows us to make a journey we could not otherwise make, past all categories of definition.

CHAPTER 11

THE EXPERIENCE OF RELIGIOUS MYSTERY

SYMBOLISM AND RELIGIOUS EXPERIENCE

With respect to the mystical tradition, one can divide the world into two great groups: one to the west of Iran, which includes the Near East and Europe; and the other, to the east of Iran, which includes India and the Far East.

Let us focus on the West. Our religions come one and all from the Levant, from the Near East rather than Europe. Zoroastrianism, Judaism, Christianity, and Islam are called the great religions of the world. In all of these, God made the world and God and the world are not the same. There is an ontological and essential distinction in our tradition between creator and creature.

This leads to a totally different psychology and religious structure from those religions in which this distinction is not made. The goal of Western religions is not to bring about a sense of identity with the transcendent. Their goal is to bring about a relationship between human beings and God, who are not the same. The typical attitude of the Levant, of the Near East from which our religions come, is the submission of human judgment to that power conceived to be God.

In the Western tradition, the divine is not within you. When you turn within, you find a human soul and that human soul may or may not be in proper relationship to its creator. The great world of the biblical tradition tells us that nature is corrupt and that a fall took place, whether you designate it as Original Sin or not. The whole concept of sin is involved here, because you have a responsibility to God to obey some kind of law that you conceive Him to have rendered.

How in this tradition do you get related to God? The relationship is accomplished through an institution. This we may term the first mythic dissociation in that it dissociates the person from the divine principle. The individual can only become associated with the divine through the social institution. Thus, in the Jewish tradition, God and His people have a covenant regarding their special relationship.

In the Christian tradition, Christ is the center because He is true God and true Man. This is regarded as a mystery because of the unity of these two natures. It is no mystery at all in the Orient, where each of us is conceived to be precisely a piece of God.

Our Western religious culture is committed to these social groups and their various biblical and ecclesiastical claims, which, in the light of modern historical and scientific research, are brought into question. By this arrangement, however, we have been emptied of our sense of our own divinity. We have been committed to a social organization or hierarchical institution, which sets up a claim for itself. And now that claim itself is in question. This breeds what we term alienation—that is, an individual sense of estrangement from the religious institution through which we relate to God.

The God of the institution is not supported by your own experience of spiritual reality. This opens a gap challenging the validity of the human being. The first aim of the mystical is to validate the person's individual human experience.

EXPERIENCING MYSTERY

As we have previously mentioned, the primary purpose of a dynamic mythology, which we may underscore as its properly *religious* function, is to awaken and maintain in the person an experience of awe, humility, and respect in recognition of that ultimate mystery that transcends every name and form, "from which," as we read in the Upaniṣads, "words turn back." In recent decades, theology has been often concentrated on a literary exercise in the explanation of archaic texts that are made up of historically conditioned, ambiguous names, incidents, sayings, and actions, all of which are attributed to "the ineffable." Faith, we might say, in old-fashioned scripture or faith in the latest science belong equally at this time to those alone who as yet have no idea of how mysterious, really, is the mystery of themselves.

Into how many of us has the weight described by the physicist Erwin Schrödinger been born that "this life of yours that you are living is not merely a piece of the entire existence, but is, in a certain sense the *whole;* only the whole is not so constituted that it can be surveyed in one simple glance. This... is what the Brahmins express in that sacred, mystic formula that is yet really so simple and so clear: *Tat tvam asi,* that is you." [8]

This is the basic insight of all metaphysical discourse, which is immediately known—as knowable to each alone—only when the names and forms, what I call the masks of God, have fallen away. Yet, as many have observed, including William of Occam, Immanuel Kant, and Henry Adams, the category, or name, of unity itself is of the mind and may not be attributed to any supposed substance, person, or "Ground of Being."

Who, then, may speak to you, or to any of us, of the being or nonbeing of God, unless by implication to point beyond his words and himself and all he knows, or can tell, toward the transcendent, the experience of mystery.

The question sometimes arises as to whether the experience of mystery and transcendence is more available to those who have undergone some kind of religious and spiritual training, for whom, as I have said, it has all been named completely. It may be less available to them precisely because they have got it all named in the book. One way to deprive yourself of an experience is indeed to expect it. Another is to have a name for it before you have the experience. Carl Jung said that one of the functions of religion is to protect us against the religious experience. That is because in formal religion, it is all concretized and formulated. But, by its nature, such an experience is one that only you can have. As soon as you classify it with anybody else's, it loses its character. A preconceived set of concepts catches the experience, cutting it short so that it does not come directly to us. Ornate and detailed religions protect us against an exploding mystical experience that would be too much for us.

There are two orders of meditation: discursive meditation and ordered meditation. In discursive meditation, such as that advocated by Ignatius Loyola, you consider some religious scene—the Seven Sorrows of the Blessed Virgin or the story of the Crucifixion—arranging it as one would a stage set in the imagination. This is a protective prelude to one order of meditation. Another order of meditation is explosive because it carries you beyond all names, forms, and concepts. And then you cannot get back. If, however, you have engaged for several years in discursive meditation first, it serves as an intermediary state by which you can get back. In places in which meditation has been practiced for a long time—in contemplative orders, for example—this is well understood.

Let us find the way to mystery through a meditation on the birth, life, and death of Jesus. In this regard, the first century question, whether Christianity was *a* mystery religion or *the* mystery religion of which all the others were re-figurements is relevant. The many symbols, such as the animals of the Egyptian mystery religions breathing their spirit on the infant Jesus—the bull of the god Osiris and the ass of his brother Set, there in the manger—suggest their early understanding that this was indeed so. So, too, in the same nativity scene, the Magi wear the hat of Mithra as they pay homage.

It is clear that, in Orpheus and Christ, we have exactly the same archetype, with the motif of leaving the physical world, still symbolized with a cross in astronomy, for the spiritual. They leave the Earth, symbol of Mother, to go to the realm of the Father.

In the translation of a Neolithic fertility rite into a spiritual fertility rite, we see the death and resurrection of the grain refigured in the symbol of the death of the old Adam and birth of the new. As I have observed before, although I do not know how to prove it, the great insight of St. Paul on the road to Damascus was that the calamity of the death of this young rabbi, Jesus, was a counterpart of the death and resurrection of the savior found in the classical mysteries. Paul also grasped that the Christian myth of the Fall at the Tree of the Garden and the

Redemption at Calvary on the Tree of Redemption are the two aspects of the two Trees in the Garden of Eden. The first, the Tree of the Fall, represents passage from the eternal into the realm of time. The second is the Tree of the return from the realm of time to the spiritual. So that Tree is the threshold tree, the laurel tree, which may be seen in its two aspects, going from the sacred to the profane and from the profane back into the sacred.

When Man ate of the fruit of the Tree, he discovered himself in the field of duality instead of the field of unity. As a result, he finds himself out, in exile. The two cherubim placed at the gate are there representative of the world of the pairs of opposites in which, having been cast out of the world of unity, he is now located. You are kept in exile by your commitment to that world.

Christ goes past that—"I and the Father are one"—back into the realm of unity from which we have been expelled. *These* are mysteries. Here is an echo and a translation into another set of images of what we ourselves are experiencing. What comes forth now with the grain, as particles of that one life that informs all things, is the revelation of the spiritual unity in all its aspects. Here also is the revelation that one life can be personified as a Deity, as in the Christian tradition, and everything comes from the Deity. But the personification is not what is important. What we have is a trans-theological, transpersonified revelation.

When one is ready to see the eternal flashing, as it were, through the latticework of time, one can experience mystery. This is especially so in artwork that carries mythological symbols that speak to us still.

All this may be observed in the surface of an ancient two-sided vase. On one side, we see Triptolemus as an old man with Hermes before him with grains of wheat. Hermes is holding the caduceus. Turning the vase, we see that beyond this, Dionysos is led by a satyr with the chalice of wine. Triptolemus is associated with the bread, the grain, and Dionysos with the wine. These are the elements of the Roman Catholic sacraments of the Mass.

On a fifth century B.C. red-figured ceramic piece, one may see the goddess with the two powers, the serpent power and the solar power. The serpent power is the bite of death to ego that opens the eye and the ear to the eternal.

There are two orders of religious perspective. One is ethical, pitting good against evil. In the biblically grounded Christian West, the accent is on ethics, on good against evil. We are thus bound by our religion itself to the field of duality. The mystical perspective, however, views good and evil as aspects of one process. One finds this in the Chinese yin-yang sign, the *dai-chi*.

We have, then, these two totally different religious perspectives. The idea of good and evil absolutes in the world after the fall is biblical and as a result you do not rest on corrupted nature. Instead, you correct nature and align yourself with the good against evil. Eastern cults, on the other hand, put you in touch with nature, where what Westerners call good and evil interlock. But by what right, this Eastern tradition asks, do we call these things evil when they are of the process of nature?

I was greatly impressed when I was first in Japan to find myself in a world that knew nothing of the Fall in the Garden of Eden and consequently did not consider nature corrupt. In the Shinto scriptures one reads that the processes of nature cannot be evil. In our tradition, every natural impulse is sinful unless it has been purified in some manner.

In some artistic representations, one sees the Deity and at His right stand the three Graces. The muses are clothed because art clothes mystery. The final revelation is the naked mystery itself. The first of the three Graces is Euphrosyne, or rapture, sending forth the energy of Apollo into the world. The second is Aglaia, splendor, bringing the energy back. Then, embracing the two, we find Thalia, abundance. One recognizes that these are the functions of the Trinity in the Christian biblically based tradition in which these same powers are given a masculine form.

Finally, it does not matter whether you are going to name them male and female. Transcendence is beyond all such naming. This symbol refers to what might simply be called total meditation. Father is Thalia, the abundance who unites the other two. The Son is Euphrosyne, the rapture of love that pours itself into the world. The Holy Spirit, the Paraclete, is Aglaia, who carries us back. The energy itself stems from Apollo, who in the Christian tradition is the one Divine substance of which the three of the Trinity are personalities.

Remember my earlier statement that the experience of mystery comes not from expecting it but through yielding all your programs, because your programs are based on fear and desire. Drop them and the radiance comes.

CHAPTER III

OUR NOTIONS OF GOD

Kant's "Critique of Pure Reason" provides us with a basis for understanding the ineffable nature of the divine. As Kant observes, all our experience comes to us within the field of time and space. Hence, we are separate from each other because there is space in which to be separate. Time and space are the profound conditioning factors of our human lives. We cannot experience anything except in the field of time and space. Kant calls this "the aesthetic forms of sensibility." This is what in India is called *maya*. Maya is the field of time and space that transforms that which is transcendent of the manifestation into a broken up world.9

When you think about what you have experienced in the apprehension of forms in time and space, you employ the grammar of thought, the ultimate categories of which are: being and nonbeing. Is there a God? If the word "God" means anything, it must mean nothing. God is not a fact. A fact is an object in the field of time and space, an image in the dream field. God is no dream, God is no fact—"God" is a word referring us past anything that can be conceived of or named. Yet people think of their God as having sentiments as we do, liking these people better than those, and having certain rules for their lives. Moses received a great deal of information from what we might call this nonfact. As understood particularly in the Judeo-Christian tradition, God is a final term.

In almost all other systems, the gods are agents, manifestations, or imagined functionaries of an energy that transcends all conceptualization. They are not the source of the energy but are rather agents of it. Put it this way: Is the god the source, or is the god a human manner of conceiving of the force and energy that supports the world? In our tradition God is a male. This male and female differentiation is made, however, within the field of time and space, the field of duality. If God is beyond duality, you cannot say that God is a "He." You cannot say God is a "She." You cannot say God is an "It."

That is why, when Zen masters talk, they always dissolve the word by saying the opposite immediately afterward. That which is no thing. That which is no that. This is the ultimate reference of our metaphors. There are then metaphorical references, connotations, this side of that ultimate reach, opening the mystery of the operation of this transcendent energy in the field of time and space.

We should become transparent to transcendence.[10] In our notions of our lives, of what is worth living for, we relate ourselves to the phenomenal forms with which we are familiar.

If we take these forms as things in themselves and link ourselves to those outer seemings, we are not transparent to transcendence and neither are the forms. The goal in psychiatry, it is said, is to bring the mental structure that is governing our lives into accord with this energy that comes from sources we do not fully understand and cannot locate. We thereby become transparent to transcendence. We become like panes of glass, and a radiance shines through us that is otherwise blocked off. A god should in a like way properly be transparent to transcendence.

When Yahweh says, "I am God," he closes off that possibility. When your God is transparent to transcendence, however, so are you. That which is of the transcendent is the same in the god as in yourself. If the god opens to transcendence, you are one with what you call "God." Thus the god image introduces you to your own transcendence. This may be somewhat hard to grasp. But when the god closes himself and says, "I am God," he closes you, too, because this says you are just a fact and so the relationship, in these terms, is between you and the fact that is no fact.

That is why, to appreciate the language of religion, which is metaphorical, one must constantly distinguish the denotation, or concrete fact, from the connotation, or transcendent message.

Let us examine some familiar religious imagery. One of the great themes in both Judaism and Christianity is the End of the World. What is the meaning of the End of the World? The denotation is that there is going to be a terrific cosmic calamity and the physical world is going to end. That, as we know, is the denotation. What is the connotation of the End of the World? In the Gospel of Mark, chapter 13, Jesus tells about the End of the World. He describes it as a terrible, terrible time with fire and brimstone devouring the earth. He says, "Better not to be alive at that time." He also says, "This generation will not pass away, but these things will have come to pass." These things did not, however, come to pass. And the Church, which interprets everything concretely, taking the denotation instead of the connotation as the term of the message, said that, no, this did not come to pass but it is going to come to pass, because what Jesus meant by generation is the generation of Man.

Now in the Gnostic Gospel of Thomas, part of the great midcentury discovery of ancient texts, Jesus says, "The Kingdom will not come by expectation. The Kingdom of the Father is spread upon the earth, and men do not see it." Not seeing it, we live in the world as though it were not the Kingdom. Seeing the Kingdom—*that* is the End of the World. The connotation is transcendent of the denotation. You are not to interpret the phrase, "the End of the World" concretely. Jesus used the same kind of vocabulary that Eastern gurus use. In their full-fledged teaching mode they speak as though they were themselves what they are speaking about; that is to say, they have in their minds identified themselves with a mode of consciousness that then speaks through them.

So when Jesus says, "I am the all," he means: "I have identified myself with the all." That is what he means when he says, in the Gospel of Thomas, "Split the stick, you will find me there." This does not refer to the one who is talking to you, not to that physical body; it refers instead to that which he indeed, and you indeed, in fact, are. Thou art that.[11]

In any of the orthodox biblical traditions, one cannot identify oneself with God. Jesus identified himself with God in this sense. But God is a metaphor, as he also is a metaphor for that which we all are. And he says in this Thomas Gospel, "He who drinks from my mouth will become as I am, and I shall be he." Not the "I" standing there, talking to his disciples, physically present before them. It is the "I" of the dimension out of which he is speaking. "Split the stick, you will find me there; lift the stone, there am I." And, of course, "The Kingdom of Heaven is within you. Is it above? If so, the birds will be there before you. Is it below? The fish will be there before you. The Kingdom of Heaven is within you." Who and what is in Heaven? God is in Heaven. Where is God? Within you.

This idea is the sense of Zen Buddhism. You must find it in yourself. You are it: "Thou art that. *Tat tvam asi.*" That message from India electrifies us, but, sadly, the churches are not preaching it.

I have received, every now and then, one of these translated collections of the mystics of the Judeo-Christian tradition, in which the denotation is consistently taken for the connotation. When these translations meditate on Jesus, that is worship, not mysticism. They are meditating on the concrete referents of the death and resurrection of Jesus.

You cannot meditate on those things anymore that way. Jesus dies, resurrects, and physically ascends to Heaven. His mother, Mary, a few months, or weeks, or years later does the same in what is called the Dormition of the Virgin, which means that she never died as we do but was carried to Heaven—the Assumption of the Virgin. But emphasizing the physical situation simply devalues the symbol because it is thereby interpreted as a concrete term.

That is why I used the phrase, "The Inner Reaches of Outer Space" as a title for one of my books. That which is depicted as though it were in outer space actually connotes something that ought to happen in inner space. The Heaven to which these bodies of Jesus and Mary supposedly ascended physically is really that to which you descend when you go into yourself, which is the place, if we are still using concretizing terms, out of which you came. And within which you are. And where indeed you are.

The fundamental, simple, and great mystical realization is that by which you identify yourself with consciousness, rather than with the vehicle of consciousness. Your body is a vehicle of consciousness.

Think of the electric lights in a room. You can say, "The lights—plural—are on." You can say, "The light—singular—is on." These are two ways of saying exactly the same thing. In one case you are giving accent to the vehicle of the light: "The lights—plural—are on." And in the other, you are giving accent to that which you are finally talking about, namely, the light.

The Japanese use two very simple terms to refer to these conditions. One refers to "the realm or world of the individual," and the other to "the world of the general." There is also a very nice little saying, "Individual, general—no obstruction." No obstruction means that they are the same.

If a light bulb burns out and the superintendent of the building comes in and sees that it isn't working, he does not say: "What a pity! That is the bulb of all bulbs." He takes it out, throws it away, and puts in another bulb. What is important? Is it the illumination, or is it the bulb? What is important and of what are these bulbs the vehicles? They are the vehicles of light, or, for our purposes, of consciousness.

With what do we identify ourselves, finally? With the bulb, or with the consciousness? The consciousness would not be there if the bulb were not there but it is the consciousness that is of significance here. When you have identified yourself with the consciousness, the body drops off. Nothing can happen to you. You are ready to be grateful to the body and to love it for having brought you to this realization, but it is only the vehicle.

What you find is that which was not born did not die but came into manifestation through this body and it is the same thing that is in the bodies of others. One can now say, "Individual, individual—no obstruction." How should this idea be understood? It is the awakening of the heart, the awakening of *Mitleid,* of compassion. Relationships are transformed from passion to compassion by this realization. These relationships are no longer of mere possession, or of combat with other people, but of identification with them. In the identification you can participate in the combat, of course, but in an altogether different mode from that of ruthless animality.

What is central to our considerations is found at that level that rises above that of mere self-preservation. There arises the awakening of compassion, the opening of the human quality in our relationships with both friends and strangers.

In Jane Goodall's work on chimpanzees, she describes an incident in which her little company of chimpanzees was afflicted by an infantile paralysis plague. Adults as well as little ones died; it was a disaster for the little community. One of the big master chimps was very badly deformed by the disease.

Jane Goodall, of course, had been experiencing the sentiment that many people working with animals do, namely, that animals are really more moral and kind and generous than human beings. We encounter the same idea in Lilly's work with porpoises.

But when this big fellow was deformed, Goodall found that instead of exciting compassion in his companions, he excited revulsion, and they would have nothing to do with him and abandoned him. It struck me then that compassion is the human possibility that is not shared at all by creatures limited by their animal nature.

It is not uncommon for us, however, to have an initial animal-like revulsion for the severely deformed. We find ourselves not wanting to go near them. We must then awaken our compassion in order to respond to them humanly.

Recall the Crucifixion and the major problem for Christianity of explaining why Christ Jesus was crucified. The atonement theory suggests that God the Father was so offended by the disobedience of Adam and Eve that their transgression had to be atoned for. The offense was so great, however, that mere man could not atone for it, and the Son of God became man in order to make atonement in some equal manner.

The idea of redemption was explained by Pope Leo the Great in this way: Man after the Fall was in the keep of the Devil. The Devil had taken hold of Man, and Man was redeemed—as you would redeem something given as a pledge of security, at a pawn shop, say—through Jesus' giving himself. The Devil could not hang on to Jesus, and so Satan was himself cheated just as he had cheated Man.

Think of that in relation to the people to whom Paul preached his message. The apostle went to Athens and they laughed at him. He went to Jerusalem and they threw stones at him and he had to ask the Roman army to protect him. When he went to Corinth, a famous merchant town, his hearers, well versed in banking, got his message. This mystery of atonement, guilt, and sin is not diminished but made intelligible because it is expressed in the metaphors of banking.

Abelard, however, spoke in a different way. He, of course, was the monk who had that tragic love affair with Heloise, his young student. He developed the notion that Christ, in suffering on the Cross, represents that quality of life that evokes our compassion.

This mystery is also the theme in the Arthurian legends of the Grail King who has been hideously wounded. The Waste Land is that territory of wounded people—that is, of people living inauthentic lives, broken lives, who have never found the basic energy for living, and they live, therefore, in this blighted landscape. That is the Waste Land, which is a prominent aspect of the Grail legend.

How are we to awaken the Waste Land? The Grail King has been injured, and with his injury in a land in which everyone else is injured as well, there is no human growth. The Grail King's injury is symbolic of the condition of the society. T.S. Eliot, in his poem "The Waste Land," describes his vision of the same situation in our society.[12]

In the thirteenth century, because of socially arranged marriages, solely because they had to, people were living with spouses whom they did not love. These were not authentic relationships. What, we may ask, is an authentic marriage? It is a mystery in which two bodies become one flesh; it is not a negotiation in which two bank accounts merge into one.

There were, however, people in that Waste Land in official positions who had not earned their roles and in no way represented the heart. They are left quite apart from it. We speak of schizophrenia, a condition in which people are split in half; we even call this crisis a crack-up. These divided souls plunge into the night sea of the realities that are down there, about which they had never known, and they are terrified by demons. You can take this precept as a basic theological formula: a deity is the personification of a spiritual power, and deities who are not recognized become demonic and are really dangerous. One has been out of communication with them: their messages have not been heard, or, if heard, not heeded. And when they do break through, in the end, there is literally hell to pay.

Myths derive from the visions of people searching their own most inward world. Out of myths cultures are founded. Consider, for example, the great myth on which the whole medieval civilization was founded. The great myth—and I am not saying that it is not based on fact, only that, whether factual or not, its psychological appeal is as myth—is that of the Fall and Redemption, the "fall" of man and the "redemption" of man. The whole of the medieval culture was a construct designed to carry the message and grace of that "redemption" to the world. But when the historicity of the facts to which the myth was attached was called into question, and the rituals through which the myth was actualized were rejected, the civilization, that specifically medieval civilization, collapsed and a new civilization arose, inspired by new dreams, visions, beliefs, and expectations of fulfillment.

Myths, like dreams, are products of the imagination. And there are two orders of dream, the simple personal dream, in which the dreamer becomes involved in adventures reflective only of his own personal problems, the conflicts in his life between desires and fears, driving wishes and moral prohibitions, and similar materials that are typically dealt with in a Freudian psychoanalysis. There is also another dream level that can be thought of as that of vision, where one has transcended the sphere of a merely personal horizon and come into confrontation with the same, great, *universal* problems that are symbolized in all great myths.

For example, when disaster strikes, when you meet with a great calamity, what is it that supports you and carries you through? Do you have anything that supports and carries you through? Or does that which you thought was your support now fail you? That is the test of the myth, the building myth, of your life.

Elements of Our Experience of the Mystery of God

A well-functioning mythology in a traditional civilization, as we have noted, serves essentially four fundamental functions, the first of which I have called the mystical function of arousing and maintaining in the individual a sense of awe and gratitude before what is, and will forever remain, the mystery of being, the mystery of the universe and of oneself within it. When you consider what is beheld when your eyes really open to the world, what is beheld is not an easy wonder to affirm. For hundreds and for thousands and for millions, hundreds of millions, of years, before eyes opened to behold what was actually going on out there, there had been life flourishing on this earth. And when eyes opened, what did they see? They beheld living things consuming each other, life living on life. The first function, then, of every early mythology was to teach one to affirm and to participate in that scene.

A basic methodological principle, to be regarded when mythology is being interpreted in psychological terms, tells us that what is referred to in myth as "other world" is to be understood psychologically as inner world ("the Kingdom of Heaven is within you"), and that what is spoken of as "future" is now. At an Anglican wedding ceremony, I once overheard the minister instruct the couple before him to live their life in such a way as to merit in the next, eternal life. Well yes, I thought, but that is not quite correctly phrased. He really should have said, "Live your life, your marriage, in such a way that in it you may experience eternal life." Eternity is neither future, nor past, but now. It is not of the nature of time at all, in fact, but a dimension, so to say, of now and forever, a dimension of the consciousness of being that is to be found and experienced within, upon which, when found, one may ride through time and through the whole length of one's days. What leads to the knowledge of this transpersonal, transhistorical dimension of one's being and life experience are the mythological archetypes, those eternal symbols that are known to all mythologies and have been forever the support and models of human life.

One of the most interesting things about the Bible is that every one of the major Old Testament mythological themes has been found by our modern scholars in the earlier Sumero-Babylonian complex: The serpent-god, the tree in the garden of immortal life, the fashioning of mankind from clay, the deluge, and many others. I think, however, of what has happened as a result: Myths that originally had pointed to the goddess as the ultimate source are now pointing to a god!

This change is highly significant, and it is one of the most baffling things about our tradition. Symbols speak directly to the psyche. One spontaneously knows what they are saying, even if the person presenting and interpreting them may be speaking a different language. He is saying, "This story is telling us of the Father," while one's heart is saying, "No, it is of the Mother." All of our religious symbols are thus speaking to us in double-talk. Since, as even Saint Thomas states in his *Summa contra gentiles* (book I, chapter 5), "Then alone do we know God truly, when we believe that He is far above all that man can possibly think of God," it can surely not be proper to think of that which surpasses all human thought either as a male or a female. In our tradition, the problem is further compounded by the image of a male God minus a wife, so that we cannot even think of divinity as transcending and subsuming sexual opposites. This image of the divine is all very psychological and socially important. As we now well know, this emphatically lopsided representation of the mystery of God was primarily contrived to support the claim of the superiority of the patriarchal conquerors over their matriarchal victims.

The next point is that that which is no "that" at all because it is transcendent of all categories, is the "essence" of one's own being. It is immanent—it is right here, right now, in the watch you wear, in the piece of paper on which I'm writing. Take any object, draw a ring around it, and you may regard it in the dimension of its mystery. You need not think that you know what it is, for you really do not know what it is, but the mystery of the being of your wristwatch will be identical with the mystery of the being of the universe, and of yourself as well. Any object, any stick, stone, plant, beast, or human being, can be placed this way in the center of a circle of mystery, to be regarded in its dimension of wonder, and so made to serve as a perfectly proper support for meditation.

Already in the eighth century B.C., in the Chhāndogya Upaniṣad, the key word to such a meditation is announced: *tat tvam asi,* "Thou art that," or "You yourself are It!" The final sense of a religion such as Hinduism or Buddhism is to bring about in the individual an experience, one way or another, of his own *identity* with that mystery that is the mystery of all being. "Thou art That!" Not this "thou," however, that you cherish and distinguish from all others.

One way to come to the knowledge of a deeper you is to distinguish, as they say, between the object and the subject of knowledge, identifying yourself thereby with the subject, the witness, and not with what is beheld. For example, "I behold and know my body: I am not my body."; "I know my thoughts: I am not my thoughts."; "I know my feelings: I am not my feelings."; "I am the knower, I am the witness." Then the Buddha comes along and says: "But there is no witness either." You can back yourself out beyond the wall of space this way. And so we come to the realization of the aspiration, "Neti! Neti!" "Not this! Not this!" Anything you can name is not it, absolutely. "Iti! Iti!" "It is here! It is here!" This oxymoron, or self-contradictory statement, is the key to what we call the mystery of the Orient.

However, it is the mystery, also, of many of our own Occidental mystics;

and many of these have been burned for having said as much. Westward of Iran, in all three of the great traditions that have come to us from the Near Eastern zone, namely Judaism, Christianity, and Islam, such concepts are unthinkable and sheer heresy. God created the world. Creator and creature cannot be the same, since, as Aristotle tells us, A is not not-A. Our theology, therefore, begins from the point of view of waking consciousness and Aristotelian logic; whereas, on another level of consciousness—and this, the level to which all religions must finally refer—the ultimate mystery transcends the laws of dualistic logic, causality, and space-time.

Anyone who says, as Jesus is reported to have said (John 10:30), "I and the Father are One," is declared in our tradition to have blasphemed. Jesus Christ was crucified for that blasphemy; and nine hundred years later, the great Sufi mystic, Hallaj, was crucified for the same thing. Hallaj is reported to have compared the desire of the mystic to that of the moth for the flame. The moth sees a flame burning at night in a lantern and, filled with an irresistible desire to be united with that flame, plays about the lamp till dawn, then returns to his friends to tell them in sweetest terms the tale of his experience. "You don't look the better for it," they say, for his wings are pretty much banged up: that is the condition of the ascetic. But he returns the next night and, finding a way through the glass, is united entire with his beloved and becomes himself the flame.

We in our tradition do not recognize the possibility of such an experience of identity with the ground of one's own being. What we accent, rather, is the achievement and maintenance of a relationship to a personality conceived to be our Creator. In other words, ours is a religion of *relationship: a,* the creature, *related* to *X,* the Creator (aRX). In the Orient, on the other hand, the appropriate formula would be something more like the simple equation, a = X.

How, in the Western line of thought, is one to achieve a relationship to God? According to Jewish thought, one does so by being born of a Jewish mother. God, in a certain period, which is difficult to date precisely, contracted a Covenant with the Jewish race, requiring circumcision and a number of other ritual attentions, in return for which they were to enjoy forever His exclusive regard.

In the Christian tradition, no less exclusively, the historical character, Jesus, is regarded as the one and only incarnation on earth of the Godhead, the one true-God-and-true-Man. This avatar we are taught to regard as a miracle. In the Orient, on the other hand, everyone is to realize this truth in himself, and such an incarnation as Kṛṣṇa, Rama, or the Buddha is to be thought of simply as a model through which to realize the mystery of the incarnation in oneself.

How do *we* achieve, however, the required relationship to Jesus? Through baptism and thereby membership in his Church—that is to say, within and by means of a sanctified social context stressing certain exclusive claims. These claims depend for validation upon the historicity of certain specific miracles. The Jewish tradition depends on the notion of a special revelation to a singular "chosen" people, in a certain place, and all these circumstances in historical time. The documentation, however, is questionable. Likewise, the Christian tradition is based on the idea of a single incarnation, the authentication of which is in the evidence of certain miracles, followed by the founding of a Church and the continuity of this Church through time: every bit of this dogma is also *historical.*

That is why our symbols have all been so consistently and persistently interpreted as referring not primarily to our inner selves but to supposed outer historical events. This emphasis may be good for the institution of the Church or the prosperity of the synagogue, but may not at all contribute to the spiritual health of the unconvinced individual.

SYMBOLS: OUT OF TIME AND PLACE

History is not, as we well know, the actual source or primary reference of these symbols. They are psychological archetypes known to *all* mythologies. That is why, at this time, the gurus and the *rōshi*s from India and Japan are having such a profound influence and exerting such attraction on Westerners, particularly young people. They are telling our flocks that the reference of these universal symbols lies within themselves. The Western institutions should understand that they are right and recall that they possess the very same symbols on the altars of their churches. We Westerners also have the same spiritual lessons in the words of many of our own greatest mystics.

To which thought I would now add another, that when you are given a dogma telling precisely what kind of meaning you shall experience in a symbol, explaining what kind of effect it should have upon you, then you are in trouble. This symbol may not have the same meaning for you that it had for a council of Levantine bishops in the fourth century. If you do not react as expected, you doubt your faith. The real function of a church is simply to preserve and present symbols and to perform rites, letting believers experience the message for themselves in whatever way they can. Whatever the relationship of the Father to the Son, or of the Father and Son to the Holy Ghost may be, as defined by high ecclesiastical authority, the individual's assent to a definition is not nearly as important as his or her having a spiritual experience by virtue of the influence of the symbol. To respond, for example, to the Virgin Birth within one's heart by a birth of the spiritual life that we know as "of Christ." This Virgin Birth within is well expressed in Saint Paul's statement, "I live, now not I, but Christ liveth in me" (Gal. 2:20).

We are all born as animals and live the life that animals live: We sleep, eat, reproduce, and fight. There is, however, another order of living, which the animals do not know, that of awe before the mystery of being, the *mysterium tremendum et fascinans,* that can be the root and branch of the spiritual sense of one's days. That is the birth—the Virgin Birth—in the heart of a properly human, spiritual life.

As the mystic Meister Eckhart declared of such a crisis in a sermon to his congregation ("Sermons and Collations" LXXXXVIII), "It is more worth to God his being brought forth ghostly in the individual virgin or good soul than that he was born of Mary bodily." [13] To which he added, "This involves the notion of our being the only Son whom the Father has eternally begotten. . . . The best God ever did for Man was to be man himself." Reading the symbol this way sheds the dross of history for the immediacy of our experience of mystery.

Just think of it! We have come forth from this Earth of ours. And the Earth itself came of a galaxy, which, in turn, was a condensation of atoms gathered in from space. The Earth may be regarded as a precipitation of space. Is it any wonder, then, that the laws of that space are ingrained in our minds? The philosopher Alan Watts once said, "The Earth is peopling, as apple trees 'apple.' People are produced from the earth as apples from apple trees." We are the sensing organs of the Earth. We are the senses of the universe. We have it all right here within us. And the deities that we once thought were out there, we now know, were projected out of ourselves. They are the products of our human imagination seeking to interpret, one way or another, the mysteries of the universe, which we surely see today as a very different universe from what it was in the days when Yahweh threw down stones from heaven on the army of the Amorites and caused the sun to stand still in the sky until his chosen nation took vengeance on its enemies (Joshua 10:13).

Nor is our society what the ancient once was. The laws of social life today change from minute to minute. There is no more security in the knowledge of some communicated moral law. One must search out one's own values and assume responsibility for one's own order of action and not simply follow orders handed down from some period past. Moreover, we are intensely aware of ourselves as individuals, each responsible in his or her own way, to themselves and to their world.

We can no longer speak of "outsiders." It once was possible for the ancients to say, "We are the chosen of God!" and to save all love and respect for themselves, projecting their malice "out there." That today is suicide. We have now to learn somehow to quench our hate and disdain through the operation of an actual love, not a mere verbalization, but an actual *experience* of compassionate love, and with that fructify, simultaneously, both our neighbor's life and our own.

There is a passage in the Old French *Queste del Saint Graal* that epitomizes the true spirit of Western man. It tells of a day when the knights of Arthur's court gathered in the banquet hall waiting for dinner to be served. It was a custom of that court that no meal should be served until an adventure had come to pass. Adventures came to pass in those days frequently so there was no danger of Arthur's people going hungry. On the present occasion the Grail appeared, covered with a samite cloth, hung in the air a moment, and withdrew. Everyone was exalted, and Gawain, the nephew of King Arthur, rose and suggested a vow. "I propose," he said, "that we all now set forth in quest to behold that Grail unveiled." And so it was that they agreed. There then comes a line that, when I read it, burned itself into my mind. "They thought it would be a disgrace to go forth in a group. Each entered the forest at the point that he himself had chosen, where it was darkest, and there was no way or path."

No way or path! Because where there is a way or path, it is someone else's path. And that is what marks the Western spirit distinctly from the Eastern. Oriental gurus accept responsibility for their disciples' lives. They have an interesting term, "delegated free will." The guru tells you where you are on the path, who you are, what to do now, and what to do next.

The romantic quality of the West, on the other hand, derives from an unprecedented yearning, a yearning for something that has never yet been seen in this world. What can it be that has never yet been seen? What has never yet been seen is your own unprecedented life fulfilled. Your life is what has yet to be brought into being.

In this modern world of ours, in which all things, all institutions, seem to be going rapidly to pieces, there is no meaning in the group, where all meaning was once found. The group today is but a matrix for the production of individuals. All meaning is found in the individual, and in each one this meaning is considered unique. And yet, let us think, in conclusion about this: when you have lived your individual life in your own adventurous way and then look back upon its course, you will find that you have lived a model human life, after all.

CHAPTER IV

THE RELIGIOUS IMAGINATION AND THE RULES OF TRADITIONAL THEOLOGY

The problem for and the function of religion in this age is to awaken the heart. When the clergy do not or cannot awaken the heart, that tells us that they are unable to interpret the symbols through which they are supposed to enlighten and spiritually nourish their people. When, instead, the clergy talk of ethical and political problems, that constitutes a betrayal of the human race. This substitution of social work, or heavy involvement in regulating the intimate decisions of family life, has nothing to do with the real calling of the clergy to open to their people the dimensions of the meaning of the Death, Resurrection, and Ascension of Jesus. These latter constitute a system of symbols that works perfectly.

Missing that simple orientation, the Roman Catholic Church, for example, has translated its Latin liturgy into local languages, thereby diluting or removing its essential mystery. When Catholics go to Mass in Latin, the priest is addressing the infinite in a language that has no domestic associations; the people attending are thereby elevated into transcendence.

But when the liturgy is recited in a person's own local language, and the altar is turned around, the priest resembles less an intermediary of mystery than he does Julia Child, the television cook. The very possibility of transcendent experience is destroyed. A person may have a nice comfortable feeling, but that is not difficult to achieve and people do not go to church just to have such feelings.

The religious symbols were, therefore, short-circuited by this process that Church authorities mistakenly thought of as progress. It is an example of the prime religious problem of the day: Symbols are chronically misread. Metaphors, the essential structures of religious language, as we have observed before and will recall yet again, are read in terms of their concrete referents, or denotations, with the result that one people is pitted against another people, when, in truth, the whole sense of metaphor is to transcend separation and duality. When the clergy fail in their first task of understanding the symbols of which they are guardians one is forced to feel that only artists are left to do this spiritual exploration for us.

Things get complicated when you move into a narrative peopled with characters. For this purpose, James Joyce turns to Aristotle and what he terms "the tragic emotions." The tragic emotion is an emotion that breaks you past the mere appearance of a phenomenon to a rapture. Aristotle called these tragic emotions "pity" and "terror."

Stephen Dedalus, who is the hero of Joyce's *A Portrait of the Artist as a Young Man,* says, "Aristotle has not defined pity and terror, I have."[14] Stephen's definitions of pity and terror are very important for any artist who deals with narrative.

Pity is the emotion that arrests the mind before whatsoever is grave and constant in human suffering. The emotion that arrests the mind, before whatsoever is grave and constant in human suffering, cannot be changed and unites it with the human sufferer. The human sufferer is the important word here, not the American sufferer, not the black sufferer, not the Jewish sufferer, but the human sufferer. Pity is, therefore, the emotion that arrests the mind before whatsoever is grave and constant in human suffering and unites it with the human sufferer.

Joyce and Aristotle define terror in a way that is distinct from fear. It is a static experience of the sublime, of that which transcends pain. It is the emotion that arrests the mind before whatsoever is grave and constant in human suffering and unites it with the secret cause. What does that mean? That is the key to the whole thing: the secret cause.

Imagine that a black man is shot and killed by a white man. What is the cause of the death? Is it the bullet? That is the instrumental cause. If you are going to write about bullets and how they should not be around, or that it is bad to have guns in hardware stores where everybody can buy them, you may be writing a very important tract on gun control, but it will not be a tragedy, no matter how you make it work. The white man shoots the black man.

Is the cause of this murder the racial conflict in the United States? If that is what you are writing about, that is also the instrumental cause and not the secret cause of this black man's death. You may be writing a very important social tract, but it will not be a tragedy. It is a calamity but it is not a tragedy.

The reason I spoke of a white man and a black man is that I am thinking specifically of Martin Luther King, Jr., and his brave words shortly before his assassination, "I know that in pressing on for this justice and this cause I am challenging death." That is the secret cause.

The secret cause of your death is your destiny. Every life has a limitation, and in challenging the limit you are bringing the limit closer to you, and the heroes are the ones who initiate their actions no matter what destiny may result. What happens is, therefore, a function of what the person does. This is true of life all the way through. Here is revealed the secret cause: your own life course is the secret cause of your death.

This also causes the accident that this rather than another event becomes the occasion of one's death. The accident that you die this way instead of in a different time and a different place is a fulfillment of your destiny: All these deaths are secondary. What must be manifested through the event is the majesty of the life that has been lived and of which it is a part. In art you do not say "No." You say "Yes." When we say, "Would that I too should die in this manner," we mean that we wish we could die with this fulfillment. Death, in this view, is understood as a fulfillment of our life's direction and purpose.

This idea of death as a fulfillment underlies the sacrifices of the great planting societies. It also underlies the idea of the Crucifixion of Jesus. This death of our example of Martin Luther King, Jr., is a counterpart of the death of Christ on the Cross, of Jesus who came voluntarily down knowing that the cross was going to be his death. We must all, as it were, enter life this way, and say "Yes" not "No" to it.

When you say "No," you line yourself up with the problems of morality and justice, and all such categories. That is not, however, our subject here. That is one step down the pyramid where we encounter the pairs of opposites. In that with which we are concerned there are no pairs of opposites, no desire or fear.

The perspective of "Yes" to life, with its cross, and with its crucifixion, allows the foreground of the event to open up to radiance. I remember seeing a Greek company perform *Oedipus Rex*. Oedipus ends tearing his eyes out, the kind of physical action that the Greeks loved. The chorus had their backs to the audience, and shortly after the display of this horror, the members turned around and opened their arms, and there you sensed that going past the human suffering to the majesty of what is contained in that play— that is, of the mystery of life showing itself through the action of life. There lies the key to art. It is beyond the pairs of opposites, beyond desire or fear. This transformation is the experience of the sublime. "I am beyond fear of the death that is threatened here."

This sense derives from departure into the Self, the art that lies before all. Through art we put aside all calls so that we may sense and respond to the metaphysical call. All religions are ethical in their foreground. But there exists a metaphysical ground beyond good and evil, beyond I and Thou, beyond life and death. When the symbol is opened, that background is what shines through and flows forth.

The function of the mythology, we recall, is also to spiritualize the place as well as the conditions in which you live. The function of the artist is to do that for you. But the artists that are responsible for the poetry of the Bible, which is glorious poetry, are not now here. Their work has been concretized. And we have this perduring and difficult notion, this corruption of metaphor, that the Holy Land, the Promised Land, lies somewhere else.

The Promised Land is any environment that has been metaphorically spiritualized. An elegant example of this universal experience is found in the mythology of the Navaho. Living in a desert, the Navaho have given every detail of that desert a mythological function and value so that wherever persons are in that environment, they are in meditation on the transcendent energy and glory that is the support of the world. The Promised Land is not a place to be conquered by armies and solidified by displacing other people. The Promised Land is a corner in the heart, or it is any environment that has been mythologically spiritualized.

Such phrases are metaphors to help you link yourself to this vast enterprise of being alive. Man can be thought of as an animal without a fixed character. Nietzsche calls Man "the sick animal," *"Das kranke Tiere."* He does not know what his job is. But men and women have such virtuosity that they can be ninety-eight different things. Each of us has a track to find and follow.

So whatever your life commitment is as of now, it involves certain daemonic relationships—that is, the one you forge with the deity residing in you. One of the big problems in the Christian tradition arises from the interpretation of supernatural grace, which says, in effect, that salvation does not come from you, but from outside yourself through some kind of ritual experience. But the function of the sacrament of Baptism, for example, is not to pour anything into you but to pull something out of you. The sacraments are an evocation, not an indoctrination.

IMAGINATION AND ITS RELATION TO THEOLOGICAL INQUIRY

There is in the Borgia Chambers of the Vatican an extraordinarily interesting picture by a sixteenth-century painter named Pinturicchio, showing the Egyptian goddess Isis enthroned, giving instruction to her two disciples. At her left hand sits Moses, and at her right sits Hermes. For it had been in the year 1463 that Marsilio Ficino had translated for Cosimo de' Medici a considerable portion of the *Corpus hermeticum,* a work that at that time was thought to be a product of the same period as the Laws of Moses, and that, in any case, employed many symbolic images already known to the Christian faith.

It employed them, however, with a difference: whereas, in Christian thinking, following the Mosaic, the deity is regarded as transcendent of the world, in the "hermetic" tradition, which was a development rather of a Greek line of thought, divinity inhabits and is the very essence of the substance of the universe. The same images, consequently, that in the Semitic line of argument are rendered in terms of a system of game rules requiring that the deity be regarded as "out there," turn up in the *Corpus hermeticum,* following game rules requiring that the divine be present within as well as without.

Every theological tradition sets up its own game rules, and no matter what experiences of a mystical or visionary order one may have, it will be necessary when translating them into speech to bring them into accord, so to say, with the game rules of the particular theology currently in play. Indeed, one of the really great problems encountered by Christian mystics through the centuries has been the conflict of these two contrary traditions of speech, the Hermetic and the Mosaic. The one that has prevailed from the fourth century onward has been that of God as a Being transcendent, not to be identified either with the substance of the universe or with one's own most inward form of forms.

In the Renaissance, however, the appearance of that translation of the *Corpus hermeticum* generated a new realization of the values of a mystical point of view that had long been native to the European mind, though suppressed since the century of Theodosius. One detects it already in the Grail tradition. It is certainly in Eckhart. The whole Albigensian movement was based on it. In fact, it has been in tension or conflict with the dominant tradition all the time. In the Renaissance it was revived boldly, inspiring enthusiasm for its mystical insights in many of the greatest artists of the time: Botticelli, for example, Leonardo, and Titian. Herein, I would say, lies the crux of our topic, of the relationship of the imagination to theological discourse.

Carl Jung has suggested, as a means for fathoming one's own creative depths, a technique that he calls "active imagination." One way to activate the imagination is to propose to it a mythic image for contemplation and free development. Mythic images—from the Christian tradition, or from any other, for that matter, since they are all actually related—speak to very deep centers of the psyche. They came forth from the psyche originally and speak back to it. If you take in some traditional image proposed to you by your own religious tradition, your own society's religious lore, proposing it to yourself for active meditation, without any strict game rules defining the sort of thoughts you must bear in mind in relation to it (such as those proposed by Ignatius Loyola concerning meditation on aspects of the Passion), letting your own psyche enjoy and develop it, you may find yourself running into imageries, experiences, and amplifications that do not fit exactly into the patterns of the tradition in which you have been trained. What are you going to do about that? Are you going to let yourself go, following your own activated imagination? Or are you going to cut the run short at some critical point?

There is, to me, a very mysterious passage in Paul's Second Corinthians, at the opening of chapter 12, where he states, "I will go on to visions and revelations of the Lord. I know a man in Christ, who fourteen years ago was caught up to the third heaven, whether in the body or out of the body I do not know, God knows. And I know that this man was caught up into Paradise, whether in the body or out of the body I do not know, God knows, and he heard things that cannot be told, which man may not utter."

What may we suppose Paul meant by unutterable things about which it is unlawful to speak? What could he have meant by that? It must be, that, as always when the mystic turns within, he comes upon realizations that transcend all conceptualization and theological game rules. Thomas Aquinas, too, in his *Summa contra gentiles,* states that one knows God truly only when knowing that God transcends and is altogether beyond whatever can be thought or said of God. He wrote the *Summa theologica,* where he engaged himself for the better part of a lifetime in arguments concerning a list of divine attributes, "the existence" of God, "the simplicity" of God, "the perfection," as well as "the will," "the love," and "the mercy" of God.

The divine, however, is transcendent even of the category of transcendence, for that, too, is a category of thought, as is its complement, immanence. I am speaking now in the way of the Hermetic tradition, which takes seriously the idea of transcendence. Something of this kind would seem to me to be implied in Paul's words about an experience "that cannot be told."

As I have mentioned, the great Indian saint of the last century, Sri Ramakrishna, would ask people who came to him to talk with him about God, "How do you like to speak about God, *with* form or *without?*" That took care very nicely of the problem of the personification of "God." "Do you believe in a personal God?" That is finally a secondary question, a question that has to do with what I would call the "game rules" of a chosen spiritual play.

Let me now remark, as a comparative mythologist whose professional career has been spent comparing the mythological traditions of mankind, that I find it extremely useful to let the mind range over the whole field, observing that what is said one way in one tradition is said another way in another. They are all mutually illuminating. Such a tradition is that associated with the great Indian god Shiva, in which a theological system based not simply on masculine deities but feminine powers as well is personified and seen in interaction with the male in the way of pairs of opposites pointing past themselves to "things that cannot be told." Here one encounters another set of game rules, often displaying essentially the same imagery, however, as that, for example, of God and his spouse, the Virgin, but in totally new combinations. These can illuminate occasionally some of the deep "unspeakable" things of the tradition out of which we all have come.

Of all the traditions I have studied in detail, the Semitic is the only one in which the game rules require that the deity is to be regarded as absolutely the other. One can only ask: "How did this singular position come to be assumed? Why did the Semites elect this attitude?"

The answer begins to appear, I believe, the moment one considers the general Semitic background in the Syro-Arabian desert as a congeries of fighting, raiding, nomadic tribes. It has been noticed that, whereas in practically all the other religious traditions of mankind the principal gods are nature powers, cosmic deities, with the various local groups in secondary roles, among the Semites generally, and the Hebrews most emphatically, the principal god is the patron deity of the tribe.

When you have a theology of the former sort, as of the Greeks and Romans, Hindus and Chinese, one can turn from one tradition to another and recognize that the power here called Zeus is over there called Indra; and there is no essential conflict. In the sixth book of Caesar's *Gallic Wars,* for instance, where he describes the mythologies, rites, and religions of the Celtic tribes, it is difficult to know just which of the Celtic gods he is talking about, since he always applies to them the corresponding Latin names. The Celts, he found, worshiped Mercury and Apollo, Mars, Jupiter, and Minerva; concerning these, he observed that they held much the same opinions as other nations.

Can one, however, imagine a Jew discovering Yahweh in the character, say, of Jove? When your principal god is your tribal god, no other tribe can possibly possess the same theology. One cannot say, "That whom you call Baal, we call Elohim." Our gods are not the same. Moreover, the laws of a tribal god are mainly social laws. Rather than the general laws of nature, known to all mankind; they are local, historic, and specific.

The main thrust of the Old Testament tradition is clearly and specifically the struggle of "Yahweh," one tribal deity, against all the other gods of the world—the nature gods and all the other national gods. Many, indeed most, of the Old Testament kings, one after another, left the ways of righteousness to worship on the mountain tops, the deities of the great nature world whom everybody else was worshiping, and the priestly scribes of Yahweh's cause railed against them for this treason. Nature is a difficult power to resist. And within ourselves, as well, nature—Mother Nature—is a difficult power to resist. Nor is she an inferior guide to virtue and to the glory of life.

What I think history has proven is that these local social laws set against the laws of nature no longer hold as a guide to conduct, if, indeed, they ever did hold. Their whole history is of fanatic violence. In the biblical religions' unrelenting thrust against the laws of the nature religions, a tension was so built up that nature was indeed imaginatively corrupted. What a pleasure it was to live for a season in Japan where no one had ever heard of the Fall in the Garden! The whole sense of the Fall is that nature is corrupt. As a result, when you are young and full of the wonder of nature every single thing that YOU spontaneously wish to do is condemned as sinful.

This brings into our religious life a type of agony that I think is peculiar to our tradition and distinctly pathological. Only in certain rare periods, of which the Renaissance was one, and in certain rare spiritual geniuses, do we find people within the fold of this tradition who have found a way to pass, often through fire, to a reconciliation of its jejune spiritual lore with the glories of the world of life.

This world of life speaks within us when we let the active imagination function. That is why it is also a bit dangerous. Gods suppressed become devils, and often it is these devils whom we first encounter when we turn inward. Furthermore, the power that has been chiefly suppressed in the main thrust of our tradition is that which in most of the world is represented in the image of the great Goddess. She is called in the Bible (II Kings 23:13) "the abomination." But the very imagery of this Bible itself is derived from an earlier mythological context in which the Goddess was supreme. Her imagery and that of the nature deities, her children, have been appropriated and transformed to accord with a strictly and ruthlessly patriarchal, male-oriented tradition, all the symbols of which, consequently, are turned topsy-turvy.

Who, for example, wants Abraham's bosom? Who ever heard of man giving birth to a woman, as Adam to Eve? There is in all of this symbol making and storytelling a deliberate campaign of seduction, turning the mind and heart from the female to the male—that is to say, from the laws of nature to the laws and interests of a local tribe. Again, as I have already suggested, it is surely a bewilderment to the psyche to have to respond to images that say one thing to the heart and are presented to the mind as programming another, opposite meaning. This paradox produces a kind of schizoid situation, and undoubtedly one of the main reasons for the prosperity of psychoanalysts today is this tangling and short-circuiting of the symbolic imagery through which the conscious and unconscious systems of our minds were to have been held in touch.

An additional misfortune for the health of our civilization can be seen in Dr. Freud himself who was just as badly infected as the Bible with what is now termed male chauvinism. The Women's Movement may have an important influence here, extending even into the field of religious symbology. Meanwhile, in the Christian fold, it has surely been a great triumph for Mary that in spite of the resistance by the bibliolatrous Protestant community—for whom Mariolatry has pretty much the same meaning as the "Abomination" had for Elijah—she has been able to advance further and further into the orbit of true divinity. Mary's Assumption into Heaven was in 1950 declared a dogma to be believed as an historical occurrence. One must also consider, as an image for contemplation, her Coronation in Heaven.

Indeed, Mary is even regarded as Co-Savior, co-sufferer with her life-redeeming Son. The line of division here between "veneration" and "worship" is becoming less and less easy to define. The game rules are perceptibly changing. Should they ever give way completely, a real victory will have been won over the patriarchal provincialism of our past *(Extra ecclesiam nulla salus!)* [15] and for a more broadly humanized future, by virtue simply of a transformation of essential symbols through the reawakened, reactivated mythological imagination of men and women today.

CHAPTER V

SYMBOLS OF THE JUDEO-CHRISTIAN TRADITION

WHAT KINDS OF GODS HAVE WE?

Before we examine in detail the deeper, vital meanings of symbols whose surfaces are so familiar that they have become static and brittle, I would like to examine once again some fundamental notions. These understandings of our ideas of God and how we speak of deities are essential to the appreciation of the richness of the Western tradition.

Two mythologies are found in the story of the Flood. One is that of the planting culture, the old-city mythology of cyclic karma—of the ages of gold, silver, bronze, iron, during which the world's moral condition deteriorated. The Flood then came and wiped it out to bring about a fresh start. India abounds in flood stories of this kind, for the flood is a basic story associated with this cyclic experience through what we might term a year of years.

The second mythology is that of a God who created people, some of whom misbehave. He then said, "I regret that I have created these people. Look at what I have done! I am going to wipe them all out." That is another God, and certainly not the same God as in the first mythology. I emphasize this observation because two totally different ideas of God are involved in the word "God."

The latter God is one who creates. One thinks of that God as a fact. *That* we say, is the Creator. We conceptualize that God as an *IT.* On the other hand, in the impersonal dynamism of the cycles of time the gods are simply the agents of the cycle. The Hindu gods are not, therefore, creators in the way that Yahweh is a creator. This Yahweh creator is, one might say, a metaphysical fact. When he makes up his mind to do something, it is promptly accomplished. This one of the mythologies of God in the Bible was brought in by the nomads who, as herding people, had inherited the mythology of the hunting process in which God is considered out there. The planting people have a mythology of God in here as the dynamism that informs all of life.

To give a sense of the real meaning of this agricultural mythology, one must examine the actual number of years it takes for the spring equinox to pass through all of the signs of the zodiac. Called "the procession of the equinoxes," it takes 25,920 years to complete a cycle of the zodiac. Divide 25,920 by 60, and you get 432. This number, as we shall see, provides the link between the agricultural mythology and the actual cycles of time.

Some years ago a friend of mine gave me a book, Cooper's *Aerobics,* that told how many laps a man would have to swim every day in order to stay healthy. A footnote read: "A man in perfect physical shape, at rest, has a heartbeat of about one beat per second." At sixty seconds to a minute, and sixty minutes to an hour, in one day of twenty-four hours the heart beats 86,400 times. Divided by two, it is 43,200. The heartbeat matches the beat of the universe; they are the same. That coincidence of rhythm was the point of the old cosmic mythologies. The latter envisioned this microcosm, or little cosmos, and the macrocosm, or the big cosmos, as resonating to the same beat. When a person tells the doctor "I've got a fever," the doctor takes his pulse to see if it registers in harmony with the 43,200 beats—that is, to find out if the patient is in tune with nature.

These numbers, anchored in the Sumerian discovery that the order of the universe can be discovered mathematically, are found almost everywhere. In the Hindu sacred epics, the number of years calculated to the present cycle of time, the Kālī Yuga as it is known, is 432,000, the number of the "great cycle" *(mahāyuga)* being 4,320,000. In the Icelandic *Eddas,* one reads of the 540 doors in Othin's (Wotan's) hall, through which, at the end of the current cycle of time, 800 divine warriors would pass to battle the antigods in that "Day of the Wolf" to mutual annihilation. Multiplying 540 by 800 equals 432,000.

An early Babylonian account, translated into Greek by a Babylonian priest named Berossos in 280 B.C., tells us that 432,000 years passed between the time of the rise of the city Kish and the coming of the mythological flood (the biblical story derives from this earlier source). In a famous paper on "Dates in Genesis," the Jewish Assyriologist Julius Oppert, in 1877, showed that in the 1,656 years from the creation to the Flood, 86,400 weeks had passed. Divided by two, that again produces 43,200.[16]

That is a hint, buried in Genesis, that two notions of God are to be found in its pages. The first was the willful, personal creator who grieved at the wickedness of his creatures and vowed to wipe them out. The other God, in complete contrast, is found hidden in that disguised number, 86,400, a veiled reference to the Gentile, Sumero-Babylonian, mathematical cosmology of cycles, ever recurring, of impersonal time. During this cycle, kingdoms and peoples arise and recede in seasons of the multiple of 43,200. We recall that the Jewish people were exiles in Babylon for half a century and could, indeed, have absorbed these notions that, exquisitely hidden, provide a subtext of recurring cycles of time in their scriptures.

The mysterious procession of the night sky, then, with the soundless movement of planetary lights through fixed stars, had provided the fundamental revelation, when mathematically charted, of a cosmic order. The human imagination reacted from its core, and a vast concept took form: The universe as a living being in the image of a great mother, within whose womb all the worlds, both of life and death, had their existence. The human body is a duplicate, in miniature, of that macrocosmic form. Throughout the whole a secret harmony holds sway. It is the function of mythology and relevant rites to make this macro-microcosmic insight known to us just as it is the function of medicine (recall the 43,200 beats of the heart every twelve hours) to keep us in harmony with the natural order.

These old mythologies, then, put the society in accord with nature. Their festivals were correlated with the cycles of the seasons. That also put the individual in accord with the society and through that in harmony with nature. There is no sense of tension between individual and society in such a mythological world. The rules as well as the rituals of such a society put persons in accord not only with their social world, the world of nature without, but also with their own human nature within.

In the course of the second millennium B.C. a strange thing happened in the Near Eastern realms, "the great reversal," as I term it. As you know, when you have people who think the world is heating up, their subjective reaction is to want to cool it off. At that period, one observes the beginnings of meditation, the effort to disengage the self from the world. Another reading of this reversal reveals the spirit of Jainism, which is based on the ideals of nonviolence. The familiar question, "How can one live and be nonviolent?" has a familiar answer, "You can't." So, the law of Jainism is to die. And not come back. This is a radical pullout from an increasingly overheated world.

Yet another reading may be found in the mythology of the Zoroastrians, those associated with Zoroaster, whose date we do not know. One view is that he lived about 1200 B.C. and another that he lived six hundred years later, about 600 B.C. He is roughly from the same period as Homer and perhaps, like him, should be regarded as symbolic of a tradition rather than as an individual person. Zoroaster was the prophet of the Persians, the people who restored the Jews to Jerusalem, the same Persians who later gave rise to the Chaldeans. The basic idea in Zoroaster's teaching is that there are two Gods, one good, the other evil. The good God is a God of Light, of Justice, of Wisdom, who created a perfectly good world. His name is *Ahura Mazda,* "First Father of the Righteous Order, who gave to the sun and stars their paths." The Mazda bulbs were named after this God of Light. Against him stands a God of Evil, *Angra Mainyu,* "the Deceiver," who is the god of lies, darkness, hypocrisy, violence, and malice. He it was who threw evil into this good and well-made world. Thus the world in which we live is a mixture of light and darkness, of good and evil. This worldview is the mythology of the Fall. In its biblical transformation, it is the Fall.

There is then a nature world that is not good and one does not put oneself in accord with it. It is evil and one pulls out or away in order to correct it. From this view arises a mythology with this sequence: Creation, a Fall, followed by Zoroaster (or Zarathustra), who teaches the way of virtue that will bring a gradual restoration of goodness. On the last day, after a terrific battle known as Armageddon, or the Reckoning of Spirits, Zoroaster will appear, in a second incarnation, the evil power will be wiped out, and all will be peace, light, and virtue forever. This mythology is surely familiar to all.

When the Dead Sea Scrolls and the other desert scrolls were unearthed at midcentury, scholars discovered that one of these early Jewish writings, called "The War of the Sons of Light against the Sons of Darkness," was sheer Zoroastrianism. The Zoroastrian influence, particularly on the Hebrew community, is represented in the work of the Essenes. We have, therefore, in the Bible itself, this concept of the world as wrong. Consequently, throughout the Old Testament one reads of the kings who, in the sight of Yahweh, do well to wipe out the nature religions. These stories represent a tension between two totally different mythologies. One is of the goodness of nature, with which individuals try to harmonize themselves. That is considered a virtuous and healthy and humanly sustaining act. The other sees nature negatively and the person's choice is to say "no" to it, and to pull away from it.

I deem this distinction of mythologies very important. We have the nature mythologies, which put us in touch with our own nature. But there also exist, one must note, antinature mythologies. These are the mythologies of the nomadic people.

When you live in the desert, you cannot depend on Mother Nature very much and the social awareness of the situation is accented. The God of this society may be negative to the desert. Among the Greeks, the two attitudes tend together. From this integration we see the reemergence of the notion of the Goddess. In India, for example, after the Indo-European invasions—around the time of the Hebrew invasion of Canaan, in the thirteenth to fourteenth century B.C.—we see a reemergence of the Goddess cult.

It is worth examining the idea of deity that is found in these Mother Goddess religions. The word "Brahman" refers to something that is beyond all concepts, and, in this regard, there are two ways of interpreting the word "transcendent." One signifies something that is out there and so transcends this place here. In that sense, Yahweh is transcendent. Yahweh is, it might be said, a supernatural fact, up there.

The other way of reading the word "transcendent" is that of Kant in the *Critique of Pure Reason,* as the ultimate mystery of being that transcends all conceptualization, beyond thought, beyond categories.

That is the notion that is found in the Upaniṣads. In India, when the female power of the Goddess revived during their period, there was some realization that the ultimate mystery is found in the mystery of one's own being but that mystery is deeper than any individual's thinking can go.

This spiritual experience has been termed Gnosticism, from the Greek *gnosis,* or knowledge, and it describes this intuitive realization of the mystery that transcends speech. For that reason, the language we use in speaking of religious mystery is that of metaphor.

Metaphor is the language of myth that remains, as we have observed, a still widely misunderstood term. Even many so-called well-educated people think that "myth" means something that is false—that is, a lie or distortion about some person or event.

But that misunderstanding arises, as we know, only when we misread metaphorical language. All of our religious ideas are metaphorical of a mystery. It is vital to recall that if you mistake the denotation of the metaphor for its connotation, you completely lose the message that is contained in the symbol.

God is a symbol. The connotation of the symbol lies beyond all naming, beyond all numeration, beyond all categories of thought. One often asks, "Is God one, or is God many?" These, however, are categories of thought and do not serve well in talking about what is beyond all speech.

You are probably familiar with one of my favorite quotations from Heinrich Zimmer, who used to say, "The best things can't be told. The second best are misunderstood." Why are the second best misunderstood? Because they are metaphors that, as we only seem to repeat too often, are misread for their denotation rather than their connotation.

Jesus dies, is resurrected, and goes to Heaven. This metaphor expresses something religiously mysterious. Jesus could not literally have gone to Heaven because there is no geographical place to go. Elijah went up into the heavens in a chariot, we are told, but we are not to take this statement as a description of a literal journey.

These are spiritual events described in metaphor. There seem to be only two kinds of people: Those who think that metaphors are facts, and those who know that they are not facts. Those who know they are not facts are what we call "atheists," and those who think they are facts are "religious." Which group really gets the message?

No good is accomplished by throwing the message out. All the messages of myth, from the period of the agricultural people on, are talking about that which constitutes the values of one's life, and of all lives. Finally, the message is right there, in this very thing that seems to be blocking you because it is taken literally instead of metaphorically. Then, especially as all the different horizons within which myth has grown up are broken, we realize that, since we are all together on one planet, we must begin to read our own mythology as something that refers not just to us, but, as in conjunction with all mythologies expressed through metaphor, to everyone.

It is of great importance to remember the cycle, if you will, that I have already mentioned. As the patriarchal mythologies rose in strength they put down the Mother Goddess mythologies. The Mother Goddess mythologies then reasserted themselves, as, for example, in the seventh century B.C. or so in Greece when they rose again in the Eleusinian Mysteries, the wonderful mystery religions. In India they also returned and the Goddess remains the principal deity in India. Kali, in one of her various forms, is Shakti, the energy that informs all of life. Thus, the myths do return in relationship one to the other.

Let us begin, then, to look again for the teeming life within texts and traditions that may seem fixed and dead.

GENESIS

It is very interesting to note, in chapters five and six of Genesis, how the priests worked out the relationship between the Mesopotamian kings, who lived for that period 43,200 years, and the ten Jewish patriarchs. They thereby united the two mythologies of Yahweh and of the mathematically worked out cycles of time.

The first part of the book of Genesis is sheer mythology, and it is largely that of the Mesopotamian people. Here we have the Garden of Eden, for this is the mythological age in which we enter a mythological garden. The story of not eating the apple of the forbidden tree is an old folklore motif, that is called "the one forbidden thing." Do not open this door, do not look over here, do not eat this food. If you want to understand why God would have done a thing like that, all you need do is tell somebody, "Don't do this." Human nature will do the rest.

God's idea, in this story, was to get Adam and Eve out of that Garden. What was it about the Garden? It was a place of oneness, of unity, of no divisions in the nature of people or things. When you eat the Fruit of the Knowledge of Good and Evil, however, you know about pairs of opposites, which include not only good and evil, light and dark, right and wrong, but male and female, and God and Man as well.

Man has eaten the fruit of knowledge of good and evil. Lest he eat the fruit of the second tree, which is that of immortal life, God throws Man out of the Garden and places two cherubim, with a flaming sword between them, to guard the gate.

Adam and Eve are separated from God and they are aware of this break in their sense of oneness. They seek to cover their nakedness. The question becomes, how do they get back into the Garden? To understand this mystery, we must forget all about judging and ethics and forget good and evil as well.

Jesus says, "Judge not, that you may not be judged." *That* is the way back into the Garden. You must live on two levels: One, out of the recognition of life as it is without judging it, and the other, by living in terms of the ethical values of one's culture, or one's particular personal religion. These are not easy tasks.

I said that God exiled Adam and Eve from the Garden, but actually they exiled themselves. This story yields its meaning only to a psychological interpretation. If you explain it as an historical event that occurred at some distant time back there, it seems ridiculous. There was no Garden of Eden as a concrete place. To believe so is to misunderstand and misconstrue the metaphoric language of religion.

You cannot even find a date for the idea of it. In the evolution of the species, did it arise with *Homo erectus,* when the human brain measured 1,000 cubic centimeters? Or did it come later with Neanderthal man, or just prehistoric with Cro-Magnon? When did this notion come?

This idyllic spot is not an historical fact. The Garden is a metaphor for the following: our minds, and our thinking in terms of pairs of opposites— man and woman, good and evil—are as holy as that of a god.

Let us look around this Garden now that we stand imaginatively within it.

What is that tree of immortal life? Even after examining in depth the rabbinical discussions of the two trees in the Garden, it remains something of an enigma.

Look closely and you may see, as I do, that they are the same tree. You are in the Garden and the tree is the way out. The way out is through learning of good and evil, a process that is symbolically expressed by eating the fruit of that tree. It is as if you are walking from a room where all is one into a room where, as you pass the threshold, all is suddenly two.

Look back at the gate of the Garden where stand the two cherubim with the flaming sword between them, and you are out, in exile from the place where all was one.

What is the way back? The idea appears to be that God is keeping us out of the Garden, forbidding our reentry. In the Buddhist tradition, however, the Buddha says, "Don't be afraid, come right through."

But what does that mean?

Of the two guardians in the Buddhist theme, one has his mouth open, the other has his mouth closed: they are opposites. One represents fear, the other represents desire.

The fear is that of death and the desire is for more of this world: fear and desire are what keep you out of the Garden. It is not God who keeps us in exile, but ourselves.

What, then, is the way back into the Garden? One must overcome the fear and the desire. "Regard the lilies of the field," Jesus teaches, "They toil not, neither do they spin." Blake, in his "Marriage of Heaven and Hell," says, in effect, "Remove the cherubim from the gate, and you will see that everything is infinite. You'll clean desire and fear from your eyes, and will behold everything as a revelation of the Divine."

All of this teaching is right here before us. In the Gospel of Thomas, which was found in the Nag Hammadi jars dug out of the Egyptian Temple, Jesus says, "People ask, 'When will the Kingdom come?'" And Jesus says, in an example of sheer Gnosticism, "The Kingdom will not come by expectation. The Kingdom of the Father is spread upon the earth, and men do not see it."

That is what the story of the expulsion from the Garden of Eden is all about. It is not about an historical incident but about a psychological, spiritual experience, a metaphor for what is happening to us right now.

The story of the Fall and the exile from the Garden of Eden is one of the two creation stories in the Book of Genesis—the older of the two. God had a Garden, the story tells us, because He needed a Garden. This theme dates back to old Sumer. In their stories, the gods grew weary of tilling the fields and feeding themselves so they created the human race to till the fields for them.

So the gods have a Garden. And they ask of Man what he is going to do besides tend this Garden. Then God makes animals and brings them up for Man to name them. But merely naming the animals is hardly enough activity for a man. God has this marvelous idea of putting Adam to sleep and bringing forth from his side what Joyce calls "the cutlet-sized consort."

That is a myth motif from a period around the ninth century B.C. In the Indian Upaniṣads the same story is found but with a difference. That which is transcendent forms itself and knows its own existence. It says, "I, Aha!"

But no sooner has it became self-conscious than it is afraid. It experiences fear. Then it thinks—for such a God is an *It*—"Of what should I be afraid? I'm the only thing there is."

Then it thinks, "I wish I weren't alone." And it swells up, splits in half, and becomes male and female. The male then begets the human race on the female. She thinks, "How could he join with me when we are of the same substance?" She turns herself into a cow and he turns himself into a bull, then she into a mare and he into a horse, and so is created the whole world.

He then looks around and says, "I have poured this forth. The world is God."

Now the difference between that and the biblical account is that God does not divide himself. Rather he cuts Adam in half, you might say, in the creation of Eve. These are two readings of the very same symbol. This twice-read symbol has its origin in a common mythology.

Turn to the *Symposium* of Plato, which is about four hundred years later, and one finds that marvelous story of the people who were like two people—that is, each one had four arms, four legs, and they went on. Three kinds of them existed: male-male, female-female, and male-female. The gods then became unhappy about them, betrayed them, and Zeus and Apollo cut them up in half, and turned their heads around so they both looked the same way. The place where the two had been joined was pulled together and is recognized now as the navel.

However, all that these creatures did was embrace each other, longing to be one again. And, in effect, the gods thought, "We'll never get any work done this way." So they separated them and put one over there, and the other over here, with each looking for the other one. This is a common myth with a single motif that is found in that part of the world at that time. It is the myth of the original androgyne.

In the Kabbala, one reads that if you live a moral life—that is to say, if your mind is in the right place and you are not a sensual person—then the person that you marry will be the one that is your other half.

God himself is male and female. The names given to God combine these male-female elements—that is, this notion of a separation and a bringing together.

These mythic themes can be regarded as just fairy-tales, or they can become illuminations for your life. And all of this symbolism is in the Genesis text when it is read in terms of its connotation—that is, the true metaphorical meaning that gives us its spiritual message and significance.

The first chapter of Genesis, a much later text, describes a different creation altogether. This text is post-Ezra, and it is after the exile in Babylon and the return to Jerusalem. Here, God creates by the word. There is, we must remember, an Egyptian text in which God creates by uttering every creation. He brings forth with just a word. That notion of the word as a sexual symbol is extended. The teeth are the vagina and the tongue is the phallus, and out of their forming words together all the gods, the heavens, and the world are brought forth. That is the God who creates in the first chapter of the Old Testament. There, too, the Cain and Abel story is probably a transformation of that first murder, or separation, out of which everything comes.

ABRAHAM, FATHER OF THE JEWISH PEOPLE

With chapter twelve of Genesis, we have Abraham leaving Ur for Canaan, where God has promised him a great posterity. First called Abram, at a very important moment in this cycle he is given the name Abraham. So, too, Sarai becomes Sarah as part of the whole transformation of consciousness that is here marked as coming about. The word "Hebrew" appears in the Old Testament for the first time with respect to Abraham,

Abraham the Hebrew, at around 2000 B.C. We call this period, and the section of the Bible which purports to chronicle it, by the name of this section's protagonists, "The Patriarchs." The stories of the Patriarchs constitute three really great story-cycles, the first of which is that of Abraham.

With Abraham the reader enters the beginning stage of the Semitic presence in the Near East. The early people there were both Sumerian, the first high-culture people, and Semitic. Then the Akkadians, who were Semites, become dominant. King Sargon became the first great Semitic emperor, and the story of his birth will sound familiar.

There was a woman living up the Euphrates River who had a little child. She did not know how to care for him so she put him in a little basket of rushes and sealed it with bitumen and set it floating in the river. Pulled out of the water by the gardener of the Emperor, that little boy grew up and became Sargon the First.

We have, of course, heard that story somewhere before. It is that of Moses. The common backgrounds are of approximately 2000 B.C.

Here we find an historical frame into which mythic and folkloric themes were introduced. These are termed "legend." First there is sheer myth in the stories of the Creation, the Flood, and the Tower of Babel. All these are pure mythology.

With the Tower of Babel one has a touch of history because it reverses the Mesopotamian ziggurat, considered those pivotal Temple-like structures in the center of the sacred circle of space, where the earthly and heavenly powers joined. These edifices did not threaten heaven, but made available a way for the gods of heaven to descend to receive the worship of the slaves of earth. We must also remember the Tower of Babel story's reinforcement of the Hebrew notion that all languages except Hebrew were secondary.

A legend is understood as vaguely remembered history into which symbolic themes have been grafted. Legends must be read, therefore, not as events that happened but rather as expressions of a symbolized idea or system of ideas.

Legend in the Bible is found throughout the Pentateuch, right through Joshua. One need not ask, "How did the Red Sea divide?" That was and is a mythological event. There are those, scientists among them, who continually try to explain the crossing of the Red Sea: "Oh the wind was blowing, the water was shallow and the sand bottom was revealed." Nothing of the kind!

In the account of Joshua, in the story of the second Moses, the Jewish people pass through the river Jordan which piles up, perfectly dry. The walls of water hold back and the whole flight of 600,000 people goes across. They find twelve stones in the middle of the river and, as the story continues, they take them as a kind of fetish. All these are mythic themes, and one must ask not, "Is this an historical fact?" but rather, "What is the meaning and the purpose of the myth? Where do we find other symbols of going through water?"

The history surrounding these episodes is all very mysterious but the appropriate question concerns the nature of the myth. How do we identify this mythological story? The myth is that of the descent of the Patriarchs into Egypt.

Joseph goes to a well. The well is dry but we understand what the well is. It signifies passage through water into Egypt and passage through water out of Egypt. Water always represents the realm below the field of manifestation, the place of the new energy, the new dynamism. It refers to the field of the unconscious, going down into that realm and coming back out of it.

Who went down, we ask. The Patriarchs went down. What came out? A people. That is the golden gem of the great Jewish mythos. In the Jewish tradition, the holy thing is the people. Just as in Roman Catholic belief, every part of the Eucharistic Host is the whole, so, too, every Jew is Israel. This very powerful mythology has held the Jewish people together for centuries, indeed, for millennia. And, as such a great story, it will continue to do so.

First is the promise to Abraham, followed by the wonderful story that Thomas Mann has developed beautifully in his novel *Joseph and His Brothers*. [17] Here Mann presents the remarkable tales of Jacob and Esau. All the parallels in that Egyptian story of Osiris and Set are found in that account of Jacob and Esau. Mann shows the parallel in his mythological interpretation of what had been a history. There was a Jacob, there was an Esau—there were individuals who would have had those names and might have lived those lives and who represent the continuity of that tradition. But the meaning depends on and flows from the mythological themes. The mythological themes are brought in to explain why Joseph is the great favorite of his father and, envied by his brothers, is sold into slavery in Egypt.

Joseph enters through the well into Egypt. Every one of these stories is of lives that are led according to what I call the "mythological imperative," because they identify the individual who is going to be the heroic leader and guide who undertakes a spiritual adventure of his own. This individual goes away into a forest, into a desert, up a mountain, and there undergoes an experience of testing, the fruit of which he brings back to others.

What was this journey with Moses? First there is the story of what is known as the infant exile, where the child is exposed and picked up by another family to be brought up thinking he belongs to this family, not knowing that his true family is another one.

One of Freud's disciples, Otto Rank, wrote a very important book, *The Myth of the Birth of the Hero*. Rank gave something like eighty-five examples of what is known as "the infant exposure." The child is born, the family for one reason or another leaves it in the woods or something like that. The child may be adopted by an animal Romulus and Remus picked up by wolves, for example—or by peasants, and will grow up thinking this is its family. Otto Rank points out that many children imagine themselves to be the children of some high, exalted family. All of the stories of infant exile show that the family that picked up the child was inferior to the true family of the child's, except one. That is the story of Moses.

In Moses' day, the exalted family was that of the Pharaoh. This family picked up the child who was from a humble home. Rank suggests that the child's true family is the one that he or she denies. The true family is the one that he thinks is the adopting family. So the true family for Moses was the Egyptian family and Moses was an Egyptian. His name is an Egyptian name, and it does not mean "pulled out of the water," although it has been so suggested by some.

When did the Exodus take place? There have been many disputes about the period. Recently, some Jewish scholars placed it about 1450 B.C., and the name of the Pharaoh is Moses. Moses means "the son of," "the boy." The significant story of Moses is that he sees an Egyptian abusing a Jew and he kills the Egyptian, and then he must leave Egypt, he must enter the desert world. There he marries and has a very humble job as a shepherd. Then the voice from the burning bush speaks, changing his life. This is the fire that is not consumed, and from this experience comes a life mission. One who experiences infant exile thereby finds his life mission and returns to fulfill it. When did it happen? There is a range of two hundred years there during which these events may have taken place. The date is not, however, what is important. What is important is the meaning of the myth.

Going down into the land of Egypt and coming out of the land of Egypt, the Jewish people become a whole people and their destiny becomes their own, rather than that of the people around them. These Jewish people come out with this strongly unifying concept of the Deity who has placed all of his will to life in them. The true sense of the myth is that the Jews are a holy people in the world.

Historical themes in the Bible became actually historical, rooted in real events, with Chronicles and Kings. These are based upon genuine chronicles in the treasuries of the royal house of David, from about 1000 B.C. Although they are historical, there is still a good deal of legend in them. Purely legendary events are also found even in much later stories. Although there is a marked interest on the part of archaeologists in actually dating these things, such dating cannot have anything to do with the early Book of Genesis, before chapter twelve. The datings can begin to handle the period of Abraham, Jacob, and Joseph but, as I have observed, one doesn't try to find true history until Kings and Chronicles. In Judges, the legends are transparently clear. Joshua's stopping the sun is a legend, not history. That the sun cannot literally be stopped does not detract from it as a legendary event, whose meaning and purpose add great value to what has been experienced by the Jewish people.

The central myth in the Bible is that of exile. Christianity is the continuation of the Old Testament. There was, as we know, a big question about that in the first four centuries of Christianity. Was Christianity a new religion? Or was it the next stage of the Old Testament?

Recall the two guardians at the gate of Eden. And the Buddha (sitting under the tree of the knowledge of immortal Life) says, "Come on through." The Jewish people think of themselves as in exile, a word very much theirs. The Christians, however, followed Jesus, who went right through by giving up his physical life. That was Paul's great realization about this young rabbi who was crucified for having said, "I and the Father are One." That is good Gnosticism. When Hallaj, nine hundred years later, said the same thing, he was also crucified by the Moslems. You cannot identify with God when you think of God as a fact. When you think of God as a metaphor for that which is the dynamism of life, and attach yourself to that, you are God.

So the Christ represents the reentry into the Garden. The Kingdom of the Father is here on the Earth. But how many Christians read it that way? The problem arose because Christianity got caught between the two influences we have described. It historicizes everything, and at the same time conveys the Gnostic message very strongly. Think what happens in Christianity about the event in the Garden. That is a sheer mythological event but it is also interpreted as an historical event. Jesus crucified is an historical event which is interpreted as the answer to that prior mythic event.

With these varying ideas of God—one outside as a fact, one within—you are pulled between a religion of identity and a religion of relationship. Judaism is a religion of relationship, that of God to His people, and the people to Him. As a member, you are not God; you are rather in exile, you are Godless. The remarkable power of Judaism can be observed in the people who so strongly experience their relationship to God through their participation in the history of Israel. The effect is that they have a spiritually informed life.

As history, Genesis and Exodus became mythologized. So when one reads them, one should not try to read them as strict history but instead as a sense of the history of the Jewish people, an interpretation of that history that accents its spiritual foundations. That is what it really is. Such a history becomes the inspiration, the image through which the readers put themselves in touch with the transcendent through their participation in this very same destiny. A Jewish philosopher of the seventeenth century said, "We come to know God not through contemplating the universe, but through contemplating the history of the human race." This Jewish history is so powerful because it offers a realization of a divine principle working in a holy people. Thus it is a God-given religion of participation, not of identification.

Hinduism is just the opposite, for in it the important realization is transcendent of all the social rules. When the yogi goes into the forest, he leaves his caste behind him. All social obligations are rejected and he is truly out of it. There are even rituals that represent the violent breaking of the caste rules, so that one can go past the society. That is another kind of religion that has recently had great appeal in America. What its gurus have said to the young is, "What does it matter what happened a long time ago? What is happening now within you?" That is the appeal that the Oriental vision has for young people.

Whether Jewish or Christian, our religions have stressed too strongly the strictly historical aspect, so that we are, so to say, in worship of the historical event, instead of being able to read through that event to the spiritual message for ourselves. People turn to Oriental religion because therein they find the real message which has been closed by excessive literalism and historicism in their own religion and which is now open to them again.

I was born and grew up a Catholic, and I was a very devoted Catholic. My beliefs, however, fell apart because the Church read and then presented its symbols in concrete terms. For a long time I had a terrible resentment against the Church and I couldn't even think of going into a Catholic Church. Then through my own study of mythology and related subjects, I began to understand what had really happened—that is, that, as it had to me, organized religion must present itself in one way to children and in another to adults. What I rejected was the literal, concrete, historical forms that were appropriate when I was young. After I realized that, I grasped better what the message was. One can do that. It is inevitable that children should be taught in purely concrete terms. But then the child grows up and realizes who Santa Claus is. He is really Daddy. So, too, we must grow in the same way in learning about God, and the institutional churches must grow in presenting the message of the symbols to adults.

I had a very interesting experience in this regard. A young Hindu at the United Nations had read some of my books and some of the books of Heinrich Zimmer about Hinduism that I edited. He was a very religious Hindu. One day he said to me, "When I go to a foreign country, I want to study their religion. I bought myself a Bible. I can't find any religion in it." It had to do with the history of God's relationship to a people, and for a Hindu that didn't say a thing. And he wasn't able to read the message out of it.

Now, the counter-story to that is the brief but interesting dialogue I had with Martin Buber when he was in New York in 1954. He was lecturing at Columbia and I raised my hand and said, "There's a word being used here this evening that I don't understand."

He said, "What's the word?"

I said, "God."

"You don't understand what God means?" he replied.

I said, "I don't know what you mean by God. You've told us that God has hidden his face, that we are in exile. I've just come from India, where people are experiencing God all the time."

And do you know what Buber said? "Do you mean to compare?" There you have revealed two sides of looking at the idea of God.

If you choose to have a God who is not comparable to any other God, then you must affirm and, as it were, stick with that God. When the God opens to transcendence, so does the believer. When the God closes, so does the believer. But then you may be face to face with something you cannot handle. The best thing one can do with the Bible is to read it spiritually rather than historically. Read the Bible in your own way, and take the message because it says something special to each reader, based on his or her own experience. The gift of God comes in your own terms. God, pure and in Himself, is too much. Carl Jung said, "Religion is a system to defend us against the experience of God." It may be a species of impudence to think that the way you understand God is the way God is.

CHAPTER VI

UNDERSTANDING THE SYMBOLS OF JUDEO-CHRISTIAN SPIRITUALITY

Christianity, as we understand, is one of the three world religions. The first was Buddhism, which began in the late sixth or early fifth century B.C. The Buddha is reputed to have lived from around 563 to 483 B.C. The earliest recording of the myth of the Buddha is in the Pali canon, about 80 B.C., set down in Ceylon five centuries after and five hundred miles away from the place of the events. It is not likely that it is very accurate biography nor in any way the kind that a modern biographer would wish to have achieved.

With Christ we have the beginning of the second of the world religions. His dates are something like 7 B.C. to about A.D. 30. I choose 7 B.C. because that was the time of the star associated with His birth, the conjunction of Jupiter and Saturn. Saturn is the star of Israel, after whom Saturday is named, and Jupiter is the star of kingship, and the conjunction of these in the sign of the fish—Pisces was extremely vivid on May 29, 7 B.C.—identifies this star as that which the story of the Magi refers. There is no reason for us to believe, however, that Christ was born at that exact time, and that the Magi came, or anything of the other supposedly historical happenings.

The third of the world religions is Islam, whose beginning date is associated with the Hejira in A.D. 622. What binds together these world religions, as opposed to those which may be called the ethnic religions, is that they are religions of confession or credo. They depend on belief, and professions of belief. Such religions as Hinduism, Judaism, or Shinto are religions not of creed but of birth. These represent two entirely different orders of religion, for the former is credal and the latter is ethnic.

Because of this credal base of Christianity, which has nothing to do with ethnic origin, the Virgin Birth motif plays a role in the life of the Savior. It does not follow that Jesus was literally born of a virgin or that He walked on water or flew through the air. The biography of a mythological savior is itself an image statement of the sense of the doctrine. It becomes attached to the personality of the savior-hero in the way legends became attached to all great figures. To take an example, consider Abraham Lincoln, who was known as a great joke teller. Within two or three decades after his death, anybody who had a good joke to tell attributed it to Abe Lincoln. So, too, the many anecdotes about George Washington's honesty. They gathered, like iron filings to a magnet, to the lore of his integrity. They stand as a cloud of witnesses to the greatness of the man and their historical accuracy is unimportant.

People with a certain value and impact of character act very much as magnets for the mythic materials that float always in the air. As they become attached to these figures, they form themselves into constellations around them, illuminating their character and their teaching. The biography of the Savior is therefore a way to find out what the teaching of the savior is. There is, however, a certain basic savior *mythos* that is in the atmosphere of human history making. This mythos is drawn on in all such cases. We can observe this story in the Buddha and Christ, the motifs of whose life stories are astonishingly close. Yet another tradition of saviors is found in India, the saviors of the Jains. There are twenty-four world savers, *(Tītankas)* or passage makers *(Tīrthankaras)* of the Yondershore. Their biographies also contain the elements of the savior *mythos* found in those of the Buddha and of Christ. Let us now examine some of these common and familiar motifs.

THE VIRGIN BIRTH

The first motif is the Virgin Birth. This myth occurs not only in the lives of great persons but in those of many far less important figures as well. The

Greek deities propagate sons on nymphs; the begettings, since the parents are deities, are really Virgin Births. In legend, this miraculous birth becomes reduced to the father's being dead. In the Celtic tradition many stories tell of the warrior or hero who goes off to battle but, before leaving, begets a son. The hero dies and so the son is born with no father and this is regarded as a Virgin Birth. Typical among the American Indians are stories of young women who conceive from rays of the sun. When the boy grows to young boyhood, he asks, "Who is my father? Where is my father?" And the mother says, "I don't know, you can't go to find your father. He is the Sun." Nevertheless, the boy sets forth to find his father. This search for the unknown father, this father quest, is a theme closely associated with the Virgin Birth motif.

James Joyce dealt with this theme very interestingly in *Ulysses*. Stephen Dedalus is in quest of his spiritual father. He knows who his earthly father is, but he must find who his spiritual father is. Who is the giver to him of his character? Who is the symbol of that ground or source of his being with which his conscious ego-system has to put itself in relation? This spiritual father is not necessarily the same as one's physical father.

There is then a whole tradition of mythologies involving the spiritual begetter and the son who must go in quest of this father. This is not always a Virgin Birth in a physical sense. The birth of the Buddha is not exactly a Virgin Birth, although Queen Maya is often referred to as a virgin. The Buddha is born from his mother's side so, again, it is not a physical birth but a spiritual birth that is represented. This Virgin Birth, as we have often noted, is a spiritual rebirth that is internal, at the level of the heart. This birth is achieved by youngsters in the puberty rites through which they die as little boys and are born again as young men. In our own tradition we have a tendency to concretize things, so that this Virgin Birth becomes a problem on many levels, including the biological. Can a child be born of a virgin? If that is not possible, we conclude that Jesus was not born of a virgin. The Catholic Church emphasizes the historical, physical character of Virgin Birth, saying that Mary's virginity was restored after the birth of Jesus, and making this an article of faith.

There is something that happens in many stories in India. The wonderful saint, Vyasa, who has been called the Homer of that land, and was more even than that, was said to have been born of a virgin. But she was a very unusual kind of a virgin who according to the story was herself born of a fish in extraordinary circumstances. (It is significant to note that Christ, born of a virgin, was also associated with the fish image.)

The occasion was a very Hindu one. Vyasa's grandfather, Vasu, had just married, and some relatives came along who were on a hunt, and invited him to hunt on the night of his marriage. In India, it is a sin not to have intercourse with one's wife when she is regarded as ready to be impregnated. They mistakenly thought that condition occurred right after the menstruation period. At any rate, just the night that he was supposed to be with his wife, his relatives invited him on a hunt, and he joined them, thinking it was his duty, or dharma, to which he was devoted, to do what the relatives wanted. While Vasu was there, in a realm of great beauty, with blossoming trees, a very erotic thought came into his mind and he had an orgasm which he managed to catch in a leaf. He gave this leaf to a bird to carry to his wife to impregnate her, but the bird on its flight was attacked by a hawk and the valuable object fell into the Ganges River where it was swallowed by a female fish who was immediately impregnated. This fish was caught by a fisherman, and when it was cut open, a little girl-child was found inside.

She grew up a very pretty girl, but she had a terrible fishy smell and, in fact, was given the name Fishy-Smell. The fisherman who had caught her gave her the job of ferrying people across the river. All of this story, of course, is symbolic. So this girl, Fishy-Smell, was ferrying people back and forth across the river. A great yogi on the boat was suddenly mastered by desire and in the middle of the Ganges proposed that they make love. She demurred, "No, people are watching on the shore."

But the yogi replied, "Oh well, that's nothing, I'll bring down a fog."

The fog descended on them and she said, "Furthermore, I'm a virgin, and it would not be proper. My father wouldn't care for this."

He said, "Well, I'm a yogi, and I can restore your virginity. That is easy." This affair then occurred and she continued with her job. When it came time for her delivery, she went to a little island and gave birth to a boy-child named, of course, Vyasa. The boy became this wonderful saint. As soon as he was born, he said, "When you need me, just think of me, Mother, and I shall appear." And he, the infant, walked off into the forest.

The tale continues, recounting some of her horrendous experiences and Vyasa's coming finally to save her. The point, however, is that this story is old and familiar, this theme of the birth from a virgin impregnated in a magical way by a yogi, or by a saint. And it is found also in the Christian legend in a prominent place. It is the myth of the birth of a great spiritual leader and it has nothing whatsoever to do with biology. Saying that, however, does not diminish but accents its religious significance. That is the connotation of a metaphor that, limited to denotation, leads to argument rather than awe.

THE CAVE

The motif of birth in a cave is also very ancient. This symbol is associated particularly with the winter solstice, when the sun has traveled to its farthest point away from the tilted earth and the light is in the nadir of the abyss. That is the date of the birth of the god Mithra, who is lord of light. He was born—we recall that his mother is the Earth—holding a rock-hewn weapon in his hand. Mithra was the principal competitor with Christianity, in the period of the first three centuries. The Christmas date was placed on December twenty-fifth, which was the solstice time, in order to compete with the Lord of Light, Mithra. No one really knows when Christ was born. It was settled on December twenty-fifth for mythological, not historical, reasons.

The cave has always been the scene of the initiation, where the birth of the light takes place. Here as well is found the whole idea of the cave of the heart, the dark chamber of the heart, where the light of the divine first appears. This image is also associated with the emergence of light in the beginning, out of the abyss of the early chaos, so that one senses the deep resonations of this theme.

There is a lovely mood about the Christian scene of the Nativity. The first carvings of the nativity scene are found on the sarcophagi of the second and third centuries. One of the earliest shows the little child in the crib, surrounded by the ass, the ox, and the Magi. Originally, Christmas and the visit of the Magi were identical. The Magi, in this particular case, are wearing the hat, shaped somewhat like the French liberty cap, of the god Mithra. They are Magi—that is to say, they are priests of the Lord Mithra. The ass, at that time, was the symbolic animal of Set, and the ox was the symbolic animal of Osiris. We recall the conflict of the Egytian gods Set and Osiris and that Set killed his brother, Osiris.

There we see the animals of Set and Osiris, reconciled in the Christ-child. These two powers, one of the light and one the dark, are united in him. They are giving Him their breath, just as God breathed His spirit. The older hero figures thereby concede their power to the younger, and the Magi, representing Mithra, join them around the new King. In that little Christmas scene, one reads the statement that the older savior figures, Osiris and his brother, Set, as well as Mithra, are recognizing Christ for who He is.

In that very earliest depiction, we already find the Catholic idea that the older myths are prefigurements of the new. That particular arrangement in that little scene could not in the second and third centuries have been mistaken by anybody as meaning anything else.

In Alexandria the cult of Osiris and Set was still in full career. The earliest depiction of the Crucifixion that we have is on the wall of a boys' school in Rome. It is from either the second or third century and it shows a male figure with an ass's head, crucified. The inscription says: "Jimmy," or some such equivalent, "worships this god." Obviously, there was a little Christian boy in the school, and his little friends were abusing and teasing him.

From exactly the same period we have, from Egypt, a depiction of Set, crucified. Set slew Osiris. Osiris's son, Horus, then had a great battle with Set. Set is not depicted exactly crucified. He is tied, hands behind his back, to the slave post, down on his knees, and knives are in him. Along with his four sons, Horus, who has just stuck the knives into him, is in front of him. Behind Set and in front of Horus is Osiris, and behind Osiris is the ox. And Set is represented as having an ass's head. There one finds the ass and the ox at the same dates specifically associated with Set and Osiris. Furthermore, in the Hebrew tradition one of the animals associated with Yahweh was the ass. It is also associated with the planet Saturn, which is the planet of Israel. That little crucifixion scene and its circumstances with the ass and the ox tells one and the same story.

THE INFANT

We have then the story and image of the birth of this wondrous child in a richly evocative setting. Let us look at other aspects of it. That there was no room in the inn is also an old story. So, too, is that of the infant in exile as the new world is born outside the province of the old. The Massacre of the Innocents is another important motif associated with the birth of the savior.

The story with the most dramatic parallel to Christianity is that of the birth of Kṛṣṇa. The world had been mastered by a great, brutal tyrant, King Kansa, who had a niece. Kansa heard a prophecy that his niece's child, a son, would slay him. So he set guard over her palace, and she and her husband were confined, and she gave birth to a number of children, and as each was born, he was slain by Kansa. Finally, Kṛṣṇa was born, and the father, Vasudeva, at night, picked him up and carried him across the river and left him on the bed of a woman who had just given birth to a little girl.

He picked up the little girl and carried her back unobserved and gave the little girl to his wife. When the little girl was heard crying the tyrant came in and picked her up and threw her against a rock. Instead of bursting, she just rose in the air and expanded into the form of a huge goddess with eight arms, Mahāmāyā, who mocked Kansa and dissolved into the air. And then he, in a great wrath, issued the order that all young boys under the age of one or two should be killed. There you have a Massacre of the Innocents.

What this story seems to represent is the tyrant king, the Old Monster, Hold-Fast, who insists on the status quo and represents the domination of the ego principle that refuses to yield and to open to the new principle, which is going to annihilate the old and be generative of the new. The tyrant must then be killed. And he is overcome finally by the hero who has grown up in exile. These are elements we have encountered before: the child exposed to danger, substituted as a child with surrogate parents, whose life is threatened by the tyrant king, and who returns to overcome the latter's power, and to bring something new to the world.

In this Massacre of the Innocents motif within the Infancy story, we find the whole theme of persecution, pursuit, the tyrant king, and the new savior who outwits him. All of this tale is very familiar mythological narrative. What it evokes, as it does with Christ, is the birth of a new King somewhere else, outside of the sphere of the powers that be, and the ultimate overcoming of these powers by this new King.

FLIGHT INTO EGYPT

The next motif is the Flight into Egypt, in which the adoptive parents are Mary and Joseph. We have also the little ass, on which the Christ and His mother ride to Egypt. We find in this legend of Christ a repetition of the history of the Jewish race in an interesting way. Because the Jews came out of Egypt, so, too, Jesus is trying to come out of Egypt. He goes then into the desert for forty days, just as the Jews were in the desert forty years, giving us a microcosmic reproduction of the great history of the Jewish race. Christianity was, until Paul came along, regarded simply as a renovation within Judaism itself, and not something for the Gentiles.

THE CHILD AS TEACHER

Normally, in such legends, young heroes engage in great infant deeds: Heracles slays serpents when he is a child in the cradle, and one after another, the heroes perform the deeds that are auguries and prefigurements to their lifework. Since Christ is to be the world teacher and the spiritual master, His infant deed is that of teaching the wise men in the temple on that wonderful occasion when the parents had to go to Jerusalem for the census. Each thinks that Christ is with the other when, in fact, Jesus is teaching the wise men in the temple. Joseph and Mary grow very anxious and ask, "Where's little Jesus?" There is a clear hero-deed motif. The wise men and the wise women at the temple recognize Jesus as the Savior. This event is followed by the little scene of *nunc dimittis:* "Now I have seen the savior of the Lord, oh Lord, I am willing to die. Take me."

We also find infant deeds in the Buddha's life, with a very strong psychological structure, much as they are in the story of the birth of Jesus. In the Buddha legend, a yogi arrives and sees the thirty-two signs on the hands and on the body of the Buddha. He says, "You are going to be either a world king, or a world teacher." So, too, with Jesus there is the idea of kingship and the idea of a world savior. The Buddha's father was a king, and so did not want the boy to become a world teacher. He brought him up in a protective environment with lovely girls to entertain him and with no unpleasant distractions. When the boy became something like a corpse and grew aware of the desires of the world, inexperienced as he was, he was smitten and had to accommodate to and assimilate them. You have nothing of this kind in Christ. Then the Buddha sees a yogi, and says, "Here is a man who has gone to achieve release from all desires," and the Buddha goes forth.

As the Buddha goes forth to the greatest teachers of his time, interviews them, and then goes beyond all of them, so Christ goes to the greatest teacher of His time, John the Baptist, is baptized and initiated by him, and then goes beyond him. What about John the Baptist? We now know from the Dead Sea Scrolls of the extraordinary period in the history of Judaism in the second century B.C. in which the Maccabean Revolt occurred. The Greeks, with their tendency to syncretism, by which they identified this god with that god, had successfully combined or harmonized the religions of the Near East. A marriage of East and West had thereby occurred and Antiochus was trying now to accommodate the Hebrew tradition to the Greek. In that century there was a very strong movement on the part of many Jews to Hellenize just as there were many reactions to maintain the old traditions. The principal reactive movement came from the Philistines. The Sadducees were far more accommodating to the Hellenization and the Jewish rulers were themselves Hellenizing.

Antiochus thought Hellenization could be accomplished. However, the officer and guard who were sent in to establish the classical Greek altar in the temple were murdered and a grassroots revolt started. This familiar story includes the transfer of leadership from brother to brother, until it came to one not of the House of David, in violation of Jewish principles. The next assumed the priesthood to himself as well, which constituted a still greater violation. Meanwhile, the Alexandrian world was cracking up, the Persians were rising, and Rome was coming in. Judas Maccabeus imposed forceful regulations on the Jewish community and there were bloody revolts against that, followed by an exodus from Jerusalem. It is thought that this was probably the period of the founding of the Qumran sect on the Dead Sea, because the dates correspond, about 110 B.C. One way or another, the situation that was developing seemed to be that already predicted for the end of the world: people were claiming the priesthood who shouldn't have it, claiming the kingship who shouldn't have it, and war, along with obscenities and brutalities of the worst sort, was found everywhere. An apocalyptic movement arose strongly, heralding the end of the world, proclaiming that the last year was coming, there would be world annihilation, and the survival only of the absolutely pure and the just. The Essene community, whose members looked forward to the coming event of the Messiah, was founded against this background.

THE MESSIAH

This idea of the Messiah as the herald of the Apocalypse was adopted by the Hebrews from the Persians. The old Jewish idea of the Messiah had nothing to do with the end of the world at all but with that king who would reestablish Israel among the nations. Some of the rabbis in the Talmudic period thought that Hezekiah was the Messiah, and that he had failed in his Messianic mission. Others called Cyrus the Great, who was to reestablish Israel politically, the Messiah. The Persian ideal was of a world well created that had fallen, and of the first man, Gyamat, whose disintegration was caused by the evil power; of a great teacher, Zarathustra or Zoroaster, who commenced the restoration of the world to goodness; and of a last war, Armaggedon, which would come in the year of the end of the world; a Messiah would then eliminate the evil power altogether, and establish a new world. This idea was then joined by the Hebrews to the idea of the national Messiah, and was taught by the Essenes and by John the Baptist.

The Essene community was located on the Dead Sea. Just north of it lay the Jordan, in whose waters John was baptizing. The rite of baptism is exactly the rite of second birth. Christ himself says, "He who is not reborn in water and the spirit, cannot enter the Kingdom of Heaven." John, who seems himself to have been some kind of Essene, had disciples who underwent a ritual of initiation by baptism, which again suggests the fish idea. Christ himself speaks of His apostles as being fishers of men. The Pope's ring carries the fish's motif on its engraving, and the early Christians were depicted as fish being born from the water, as little fish drawn out by the fisherman. We also have the baptism motif of Christ Who descends into the waters and is reborn again.

Whatever message John was preaching, it does not necessarily follow that when he said, "I come to preach one the latches of whose shoes I am unworthy to loose," that he referred specifically to Jesus Christ. What he meant was the Messiah. When Jesus came He was the one who finally received the designation of the Christian community as the Messiah. We do not know what he learned from John. There were later Christian sects who regarded Jesus as having become the Savior, having become the Messiah, at the time of his baptism by John. The heavens open, in the scriptural account, and the voice says, "This is my beloved son in whom I am well pleased." Understood metaphorically, this story tells us that Mary did not give literal Virgin Birth to a savior, but that she gave normal birth to Jesus, who became the vehicle of the *Logos* at that particular moment. This event is matched later by the departure of the *Logos,* at that very moving moment when Christ on the cross asks, "My God, my God, why hast thou forsaken me?" In that moment God did forsake him, and all that died was Jesus again, not the Christ, on the cross. That interpretation was offered by the Nestorians, who, following Nestorius, Bishop of Constantinople (circa A.D. 428–431) asserted the manhood of Christ, questioning the divinity of the infant Jesus because it seemed to make Mary a goddess.

The next development demands our attention. After having gone to the greatest teacher, Jesus departs into the wilderness by himself. This journey parallels that of the Buddha, who, after having studied with one after another of the masters, departed on his own quiet quest. Christ is forty days in the desert, and during this interval He undergoes the Great Temptation.

Recall the significance of Milton's choice in *Paradise Regained* to identify Redemption not with the Crucifixion but with Christ's overcoming the temptations in the desert. Rejecting and triumphing over the temptation of the world symbolized Christ's transcendence of the realm of Herod and his earthly rule. Christ rejects living by economics alone, the course of political triumph, and the inflated spiritual self that would dazzle others with its power. Christ responds to the last seductive invitation by saying to the Devil, "Do not tempt the Lord thy God." In other words, stay on the ground, and do not think you are purely spiritual and do not forget that you are spiritual and material.

Having overcome those three Temptations, Christ achieves His realization—that is, His awareness of who He is, although we are not told of the actual achievement of realization in the way that we are with the Buddha. The Buddha's tempter, as we have observed, was the Kama Mara, the Sanskrit words meaning lust and death. Tempted to social duty, or political action, the Buddha finally simply touched the ground with his fingertips and the Earth Goddess herself said, "This is my beloved son, who through many lifetimes has so given of himself that there is nobody here, he has a right to this spot." The army of the tempter was dispersed, and that night the Buddha achieved illumination under the *bodhi* tree.

In both cases, we observe the savior going beyond the highest spiritual teachers of the day, overcoming the tempter, who represents psychological commitments and blockages, coming to his illumination, and then going forth to teach. We see that Christ, after His days in the desert, returns to the world and immediately begins to appoint His apostles as fishers of men.

This narrative, as we have suggested, is evocative of the orphic tradition which has to do with the fishing of souls and the idea that the world in which we live is, in a way, the waters of the sea. Water's capacity to reflect in reverse the forms of the heavenly world gives us a basic sense of this symbol, so that we can conceive of living in a mirror world—that is to say, that in it everything is the reverse of what is in Heaven. The savior pulls us out of this realm and into the realm of true and valid light and experience. There is, we observe again, a strong fisher motif in all these stories, linked in several ways to the Christ image.

MIRACLES

We now look briefly at the Miracles, such as Christ's walking on water. Many of these repeat the miracles of Elijah and Elisha, as one can easily discover by rereading those chapters concerning them in the Old Testament. There we find the same miracles, including resurrecting the dead, healing the sick, and walking on water. The Buddha also walks on water on a number of occasions, and these accounts bring to mind an illuminating Indian anecdote about walking on water.

A pupil came late one day to his guru, who said, "You're late. Why so?"

The pupil said, "Well, I live on the other side of the river, and the river is in flood, and I just couldn't get here. I couldn't come across the ford, as I usually do, and there's no bridge, as you know, and there's no boat."

"Well," said the guru, "How did you get here?"

He said, "Well, I just thought, 'My guru is the vehicle of light. It is as though there were no one there, he is just a carrier of light. I will meditate on my guru, I will erase myself as he has erased himself, and I will walk across the water.' So, I said, 'Guru, guru, guru,' and here I am."

Well, the guru of course thought, "How extraordinary." The student left but the guru couldn't get the story out of his mind. He thought, "Well, I'm going to try this," and he went down to the river, and making sure that nobody was watching this curious experiment, he withdrew himself into one point of meditation, and saying, "I, I, I," walked into the water and drowned.

The sense of this story and of the miracles is that as the spirit blows over the waters, so anyone who has entirely spiritualized himself can do the same. This kind of spiritual inflation is precisely that which Christ Himself overcame, when carried up on the top of the mountain by the tempter. Christ deliberately rejects showy demonstrations of external power in favor of something deeper.

In any case, the Miracles in the Christ legend are standard ones. It does not follow that they did not happen, because it is certain, as it has been demonstrated time and time again, that miraculous cures can be achieved through people of great spiritual realization. Much of what troubles people is purely psychological anyhow, and thus they respond to spiritual interventions. Many cures of psychological illness may take place because of the influence of spiritually enlightened persons. Miracles may be functions, therefore, of deep spirituality.

Among the miracles in the scriptures, there are many concerning loaves and fishes and, as we have noted, the fishers of men motif. We also observe the baptism involving the fish motif, and so it is not too remarkable that the Christ is associated with the fish, and that on Fridays the Catholic Church formerly required a fish meal, Friday being Freya's day, or Venus's day, whose creature is the fish. If we examine all of these along with the image of the star and the other symbols, we understand that the story of Christ is told in metaphorical, mythological terms, right from a very early date.

THE LAST SUPPER

We come then to the great matter of Christ's ultimate experience of the Last Supper and Crucifixion.

It is striking to observe the placing of the Easter and the Passover festivals together on the date that had been that of the death and resurrection of Adonis—that is, around the twenty-fifth of March. The cave in which Christ is supposed to have been born in Bethlehem was also the cave of the birth of Adonis. The Christian and Greek religions and mythologies are individually oriented, and in them individuals identify themselves and their salvation with a specific hero figure, Adonis or Christ or some other.

In the Jewish tradition, however, one finds no such figure. There one observes the legend of the passage of the Jews into Egypt, and the coming of the Jews out of Egypt. When they come out of Egypt, however, they come through water, by passing through the Red Sea. We recall that they entered Egypt through Joseph going into a well. Even though the well is dry, it nevertheless is a well, a water source. Thus we discover the going into water and the coming out of the water, the baptism theme and the fish theme. The whole familiar constellation of symbols is there.

Who comes out of the water? And, who went into the water? Who went into the water were the patriarchs. Who came out, were the people. And Moses is not the hero; the people, the Jewish people, are the hero. Moses is the guide of the people, who himself does not enter the Promised Land. It is characteristic of the Hebrew tradition that the sacred thing in the world, the precious, holy thing, should be the Jewish race. And birth into that race is, as we have noted, the great, good fortune. In the Greek and Christian traditions, it is not that one is of a race, it is rather that one is an individual who has achieved a certain transformation of the psyche through a form of confession. This latter is a psychological transformation, placing clear stress on the individual.

The sense of these motifs is essentially the same: The emergence of the new thing, the new being, from the land of mud. Egypt was considered the land of mud, the land of the flesh, as parts of Egypt constitute the abyssal realm in the Hebrew tradition. From it wisdom comes as well as pain, and the Jews emerged from Egypt as the jewel emerges from the depth, and as the savior emerges from the tomb. So Passover, and Easter, and the resurrection of Adonis are all symbolic of the birth of the self-image out of the earlier darkness.

JUDAS

In the biblical legend, and in the Jain legends, one always comes upon the counterplayer to the hero figure. And there is at the end a reconciliation. The counterplayer, too, is saved. In the Christian legend, Judas is held apart.

One could, however, look at that Last Supper scene in a very different way from the way it is usually done. When Christ takes the bread, dips it into the dish, and says, "He to whom I hand the sop will betray me," is that a prophecy or an assignment? I think it is an assignment. It also suggests that the one eligible for that assignment was the most developed of the lot—that is, the one who really understood the sense of what was happening. Judas is the midwife of salvation, the counterplayer to Christ. He is the one who delivers Him to His death, and himself then dies in shadow. He is the Christ's shadow. In the Christ figure, we have this shadow motif all the time, the counterplayer against the light of the world. You cannot have light without the shadow; the shadow is the reflex of the figure of light.

There is another interesting thing about the little company of apostles chosen by Christ. Remember that he said to St. Peter, "St. Peter, you do not understand spiritual things, I will make you the head of my church." The same thing occurs in the Buddha legend. The role of Ananda, the cumbersome body servant of the Buddha, his relative, and a charming person, as with St. Peter, is that of the one who never gets things quite right, and who is made the head of the church.

There is also in the Buddha tradition the third figure, who is a smith. The smiths are considered magicians, men of great power because they can transmute stone into metal. He invites the Buddha to have a meal of pork with him, and the Buddha dies of that meal.

You may recall the myths, taboos, and rituals that concern pigs. Adonis was killed by a boar that gored him, as Osiris was killed by Set when Set was out hunting a boar, and the lance that pierced Christ's side has been equated by many with the boar's tusk because piercing His side was a completely superfluous act. So the Buddha was killed by a boar, by the pig. In these symbols, the continuity of the elements of the traditions clearly comes through.

CRUCIFIXION

What, it must be asked, is the ultimate meaning of this Crucifixion itself? Why did Christ have to die? There were two principal interpretations in the medieval period.

Gregory the Great's view was that the Devil was thereby tricked.

When Man fell to the Devil, the Devil came to hold a legal claim over Man, breaking up the tradition of creation. How is God going to get Man back? The theological notion is that God offered his own son in exchange for Man's soul. That is the Redemption. Through it God redeems a bet, as one would say about something that was lost, "I'm going to redeem it." God bought Man's soul by giving the Devil Christ instead, but the Devil could not hold Christ because Christ is incorruptible and so the Devil was cheated.

Perhaps you have seen that little drawing which appeared in a twelfth-century work by a nun. It is of God fishing, and his fish line is made up of the kings of Israel, and the hook is the crucifix, with Christ on it. And the Devil to be caught is the Leviathan, the great fish. Thus, the first Redemption theory: Christ as the bait, the cross as the hook, and the Devil cheated.

The second theory is that God the Father was so greatly offended by the sin of Adam and Eve that atonement had to be made for it. The only atonement that would be equal to the terrible sin would be rendered by God himself, because Man was unready to atone to the extent required. So Christ became a man so that Man could atone as God, through Him, and then receive the benefits from this atonement that Christ himself could not use. He passes them on to mankind. We have in this theory the vicarious atonement and the benefit for mankind through Christ himself.

THE CROSS

Why, we now may ask, has this particular sign become the mark of a Christian church? Let us ask somebody who knows—a member, say, of the congregation. His reply will very likely be that the sign is a reference to an historical event: the Crucifixion of Jesus, who was the founder of the religion represented in the church building that is here displaying a cross on its top. That is one way of reading symbolic forms, as references to significant historical events.

But why, or in what way, are these incidents significant? What was it that was so significant about this particular historical event, the nailing to a cross of this historical personage, condemned to death by his community for the sin of blasphemy? Crucifixion was a common form of punishment in those days. What was it about this case that transformed its sign from one betokening shame and disgrace to one befitting the designation of a church?

There is a great mythology associated with this particular crucifixion, namely, that of the redemption of mankind from the mortal effects of a calamitous event that occurred, according to report, long ago in a very distant period, when a serpent talked. The first man—the first example of the species *Homo sapiens*—had been forbidden by his creator to eat the fruit of a certain tree. Satan in the form of a snake tempted him—or rather his wife, who had been lately fashioned from one of his ribs—to eat of this forbidden tree. The couple ate, and thereupon both they and their progeny, the whole of the human race, were taken by the Devil in pawn. They could gain redemption only by the miracle of God himself in the person of his Eternal Son, Second Person of the Blessed Trinity, becoming incarnate in the person of that earthly Jesus who was crucified, not really for blasphemy but in order to redeem mankind from the Devil. According to this reading, the purpose was to palliate the Creator's wrath by atoning through death for the heinous offense of that primal human act of disobedience.

Clearly, the historical reading of the emblem has here become anomalous, not to say even bizarre, what with a talking serpent, a devil, and an incarnate god entering into the action. Such are not the characters of a readily credible history. The question becomes further complicated once we notice, and take into account, the fact that in the jungles of Guatemala there stands at Palenque a Mayan temple known as the "Temple of the Cross," where there is a shrine exhibiting for worship a cross that is mythologically associated with a savior figure, named by the Mayans Kukulcan, and by the Aztecs Quetzalcoatl. That name is translated "Feathered Serpent," suggesting the mystery of a personage uniting in himself the opposed principles represented in the earthbound serpent and the released flight of a bird.

Moreover, as the scriptures related to this figure tell us, he was born of a virgin, died and was resurrected, and is revered as some sort of savior who will return as in a Second Coming. All this mythos adds another, very troublesome, dimension to our problem of interpreting the symbolic form of the cross, since it must now be recognized, not simply or singly as a reference within one tradition to one historical event, but as a sign symbolically recognized in other traditions as well, and in significant association, moreover, with a number of related symbolic themes.

The figure of the Feathered Serpent linked with the Cross, for example, immediately suggests our own biblical Eden/Calvary continuity. Furthermore, on top of the Mayan cross there is a bird sitting, the quetzal bird, and at the base there is a curious mask, a kind of death mask. A number of paintings of the Crucifixion from late medieval times and the early Renaissance period show the Holy Spirit above, in the form of a dove, and beneath the foot of the cross, a skull. The name of the hill of the Crucifixion, as we all know, was, in Aramaic, Golgotha, and in Latin, Calvary, both of which words mean "skull." We do not know what interpretation the Mayans gave to their death mask; but in medieval Christian legend, the skull out of which the cross appeared to have grown, as a tree from its seed, was said to be Adam's. When the blood of the crucified Savior fell upon it from His pierced hands and feet, the First Man was, so to say, retroactively baptized, and with him the whole human race. Had there been no Tree of the Fall, there would have been no Tree of Redemption, no Holy Rood, as the Cross was called in the Middle Ages.

The answer, therefore, to our question as to why the crucifixion of Jesus holds such importance for Christians implies a complex of essential associations that are not historical at all, but are rather mythological. For, in fact, there never was any Garden of Eden or serpent who could talk, nor solitary pre-pithecanthropoid "First Man" or dream like "Mother Eve" conjured from his rib. Mythology is not history, although myths like that of Eden have been frequently misread as such and although mythological interpretations have been joined to events that may well have been factual, such as the crucifixion of Jesus.

Let us therefore examine further the mythological aspect of this symbolic form.

Those familiar with Germanic myth and folklore will recall that in the

Icelandic *Edda* (specifically, in *Hāvamāl*, verses 139–140 and 142) it is told that All-Father Othin, to acquire the Wisdom of the Runes, hung himself for nine days on the world tree, Yggdrasil.

> *I ween that I hung of the windy tree,*
> *Hung there for nights full nine;*
>> *With the spear I was wounded, and offered I was,*
> *To Othin, myself to myself,*
>> *On the tree that none may ever know*
> *what root beneath it runs.*
>> *None made me happy with loaf or horn,*
> *And there below I looked;*
>> *I took up the runes, shrieking I took them,*
> *And forthwith back I fell.*
>> *Then began I to thrive, and wisdom to get,*
> *I grew and well I was;*
>> *Each word led me on to another word,*
> *Each deed to another deed.* [18]

No one can miss the parallels here to the Gospel themes of Jesus' three hours on the Cross (3 x 3 = 9), the spear in his side, his death and resurrection, and the boon of redemption thereby obtained. The phrase "and offered I was/To Othin, myself to myself" is interesting in the light of the Christian dogma of Christ and the Father as One.

Moreover, on top of Yggdrasil, this "Holy Rood" of Othin's suffering, an eagle is perched, like the quetzal bird on the top of the cross at Palenque, while at its roots a "worm" or dragon gnaws. The latter, Nithhogg by name, corresponds there to the earthbound serpent aspect of Quetzalcoatl, the savior. There is, further, a wonderful squirrel named Ratatosk ("Swift-Tusked"), who is continually running up and down the trunk, reporting to the eagle above the unpleasant things that the dragon is saying about him, and to the dragon below the abusive sayings of the eagle. In a humorous way this image suggests a psychological process that C. G. Jung has termed "the circulation of the light," from below to above and above to below—that is, the point of view of the unconscious conveyed to consciousness, and of consciousness to the unconscious. There are, still further, four deer perpetually rotating around Yggdrasil, nibbling its leaves with necks bent, like the four seasons of the year around the ever-living Tree of Time, eating it away; and yet it continually grows.

Yggdrasil, like that other tree, is ever dying and simultaneously increasing. It is the pivotal tree of the universe, from which the four directions radiate, revolving as spokes of a wheel. And so, too, Christ's Cross has been represented symbolically as at the center of a mandala, just as in the Old Testament image of Genesis 2:8–14, Eden is described as with "the tree of life in the midst of the garden, and the tree of the knowledge of good and evil," and with a river, moreover, that divides and becomes four rivers, flowing in four directions.

Jung interpreted mandala symbolism as grounded in what he identified as the four basic psychological functions by which we apprehend and evaluate all experience. These are sensation and intuition, which are the apprehending functions, and thinking and feeling, which are the functions of judgment and evaluation. A life governed by prudent forethought may be undone by the upsurge of feeling, just as one swayed by feeling may, for a lack of prudent forethought, be carried, one day, to disaster. ("Never go out with strangers!") The cruciform diagram below makes it evident that in this view of Jung's "four functions" we are dealing with the claims and forces of two pairs of opposites; for as feeling and thinking are opposed, so too are sensation and intuition.

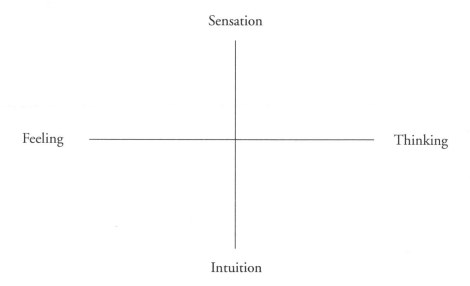

People aware only of the information transmitted by their senses—that is, of only the most obvious actualities immediately present, may be disappointed or undone by unrecognized implications. Others, intuitive always of possibilities and implications, may be knocked down by a hard and present fact. In Jung's view, based on his work with patients, we tend to favor in the shaping of our lives but one of the two functions of each pair. These may be sensation and thinking, which would leave intuition and feeling undeveloped. Any activation of the unattended functions tends to be experienced as threatening and is resisted. Moreover, since the resisted functions are undeveloped—"inferior," as Jung terms them—they are alien to people's understanding both of themselves and of their world. Whenever they do break through, they overthrow controls and with compulsive force take over with the result that the individual is "beside himself," out of control.

It is evident, then, that in our daily living we are but half persons and that all societies actually favor and foster such a fractioning through their moral assignments of our thoughts, words, and deeds either to the vice side or to the virtue side of their ledgers. Thus in the Christian system of symbolic forms, where the Cross is central, Heaven is above, to which the good go, and Hell below, to which the wicked are assigned. On Calvary, however, the Cross of Jesus stood between those of the good thief and the bad, the first of whom would be taken up to Heaven, and the latter sent down to Hell. Jesus Himself would descend into Hell before ascending into Heaven since, in His character as total Man, eternal as well as historical, and transcendent thus of all pairs of opposites (male and female no less than good and evil, as was Adam before the Fall and before Eve had been taken from his rib), He transcends in His being all terms of conflict whatsoever, even that of God and Man. As Paul declared to the Philippians (Phil. 2:6–11), "though in the form of God, he did not count equality with God a thing to be grasped [or 'held to'], but emptied himself, taking the form of a servant, being born in the likeness of men. And being found in human form he humbled himself and became obedient unto death, even to death on a cross. Therefore God has highly exalted him and bestowed on him the name which is above every name, that at the name of Jesus every knee should bow, in heaven and on earth and under the earth, and every tongue confess that Jesus Christ is Lord, to the glory of God the Father."

In this beautiful passage Paul gives an interpretation of the Savior as the one uniting, as True God and True Man, encompassing eternal and temporal terms, transcending (not "grasping"), yet to be known as both: as Christ, Second Person of the Trinity, and as Jesus, a once-living man, who was born and died in Palestine. Nailed to the cross as a living historical man being put to death, He transcends death as He transcends life. The symbolism is obvious: To His left and right are the opposed thieves, and He himself, in the middle, will descend with one and with the other ascend to that height from which He has already come down. Thus Christ is bound to neither of the opposed terms, neither to the vertical nor to the horizontal beam of His cross, though historically he is indeed bound, even crucified, as we all are in our lives. We, however, through faith in His image, are unbound and "saved."

If we read this metaphor of crucifixion in the psychological terms suggested by Jung's designation of sensation and intuition, feeling and thinking, we may recognize that in our living, in our temporal, historical living, we are bound either to one or the other of the opposed terms of each pair, and hence to a knowledge or idea of good and evil that commits us to living as partial human beings. It follows that to be released from this limitation one must in some sense die to the laws of virtue and sin under which one lives in this world, opening oneself to a circulation of energy and light through all four of the functions, while remaining centered in the middle, so to say, like the Tree of Life in the garden, where the rivers flow in four directions; or like the point of intersection of the two beams of the cross, behind the head of the Savior, crowned with thorns. "Our old self," states Paul, "was crucified with him so that the sinful body might be destroyed.... For sin will have no dominion over you, since you are not under law but under grace." (Rom. 6:6 and 14)

Hinduism, like Judaism, is an ancient religion of race, caste, or birth, and there, too, a phallic symbolism is recognized, the lingam and yoni (symbolized male and female organs) appearing in the central sanctuaries of temples, whereas Buddhism, which, like Christianity, is a credal religion of belief and faith, not of birth and race, the central symbol is that of the savior with the accent on his illuminated head.

The horizontal beam of the specifically Christian cross is fixed, not at the middle of the vertical beam, but higher, at the level of the Savior's head. At the middle, it would have crossed at the genitals and thereby have represented a phallic centering, like that of Yahweh's Old Testament law for those circumcised in the Covenant, where the religion is of race; whereas the Christian is of faith, belief, the mind and heart, to which members of any race whatsoever may be joined.

The End of the World

The Kingdom is here, right before our eyes—that is the message of Jesus in the Gospels. In Mark, the End of the World sounds like something that is still to come, a future event. Jesus is supposed to have said, "This generation will not pass away before these things will come to pass." And that was thought to predict the imminent End of the World.

People found, of course, that the world did not end and it came to be regarded, as they say, as "the great nonevent." But institutional churches still say that it is going to happen. You cannot, however, read this notion of the End of the World historically as something fundamentally in the calendar of time. If you see that the Kingdom of the Father is spread upon the earth while others do not see it, the End of the World has come for you. For the world as it was for you has indeed ended.

You see the world's radiant joy and you say "Yes" to it all and you do not say "No" to it at all. This Gnostic insight carries into the experience that we have already described of the planting mythologies. Therein one identifies or recognizes the dynamism of life in all things. We are not to become attached to the mere phenomenal aspect of the world but to see directly to its core.

CHAPTER VII

QUESTION PERIOD

Listening to a question period after one of Joseph Campbell's lectures was an enriching and, to some degree, a frustrating experience. Questions allowed Campbell to explore—in that generous, unreserved manner that was so characteristic of him—themes that struck chords in his listeners. With twinkling eyes to match his Irish good humor, he would tap into the reservoir of his knowledge and associations, enlightening the audience but also giving them a glimpse of the overflowing store of his learning. This was like the scriptural vessel of oil which, despite the books he wrote, the lectures he gave, and the questions he answered, seemed ever fresh and undiminished. Therein lay the frustration, for often even his distractions hinted at understandings and insights that, given the constraints of the field of time, could never be fully explored. These questions, taken from various periods that followed differing presentations of the lectures drawn together in this book, suggest the flavor of those memorable experiences. So, too, the answers reveal Campbell, as he was in those moments, energized, eager to respond, easily moving to associated ideas, unselfconsciously nourishing and entertaining the audience with a personal substance and wisdom that grew greater rather than less as they were given away.

QUESTION: Can you explain what you mean by the "problem" of mythology in our time?

A mythological image is one that evokes and directs psychological energy. It is an energy-evoking and energy-directing sign. A mythology is a system of affect or emotional images; these representations themselves produce this emotion or affect.

Our own mythology, yours and mine, is our particular heritage of affect images. Look, however, at what has been done to our mythology. On the rational level, the images are said to be absurd and, therefore, to have no meaning. Our rational system thus breaks their connections and makes their energy unavailable to us, in our lives.

Secondly, our symbols have been rendered neutral by institutional religions that interpret these symbols historically. Symbols that address the mystery of the psyche or soul have been interpreted, instead, as references to actual historical events which, as modern scholarship tells us, did not occur. As long as people could think that there had been a Garden of Eden with a serpent that spoke to Adam and Eve and that in that Garden an incident resembling a Fall occurred making necessary a Redemption to restore us, and as long as people could think that there had been a world Flood, a Tower of Babel, an Abraham, an Exodus from Egypt, an edition of the Ten Commandments entrusted physically to Moses on the top of Mt. Sinai, followed by a second edition delivered to him after he had broken up the tablets of the first: As long as people could conceive of and accept these things as historical events, they could also accept these symbols and move with them through their churches and temples, as well as their religious traditions. As soon, however, as people begin to realize that it is very dubious that these events ever took place, the symbols lose their historical character and their emotional energy is thereby depleted and diminished.

Thirdly, when Freud told the world that these symbols really refer to mother, father, and the little boy, they were separated from their original reference points in the mythological tradition.

There are mythologies that are scattered, broken up, all around us. We stand on what I call a terminal moraine of shattered mythic systems that once structured society. They can be detected all around us. You can select any of these fragments that activate your imagination for your own use. Let it help to shape your own relationship to the unconscious system out of which these symbols have come.

When you go along this path, you catch sight of the ox, the aspect of Yahweh that Moses saw on Mt. Sinai. It is a difficult task, however, to catch the ox. And then, the ox is gone and it is only you standing there. Next, everything is gone. This is the transcendent. In this rapture, nature begins to return. This is completed by the final step by which you return to the city with abundance overflowing your hands. Entering the city with bliss-bestowing hands, you give advice to the young people who are about to start their own search for an ox.

QUESTION: Does the mythic motif of the "Hero's Journey" apply to the Judeo-Christian tradition?

Let us review some of the basic mythological heroes who work through for us the crisis of resolution by which the classical mythological cycle is completed.

We begin with Moses, the symbol of one who goes off alone, leaving his people only to return with a law for them. This is the identical hero journey that we find in all of the old ethnic traditions. Every one of the social orders is finally traced back to the realization and experience of some single individual who alone experiences the mystery, passes the test, as it were, and returns with a message for mankind, as in the case of Moses, his coming down from the mountain with the Ten Commandments.

The next great figure in this tradition is Christ. How was Christ understood by the original Christians, all of whom were Jews? The key word is found in Paul who wrote to the Galatians that Christ redeemed man from the curse of the Law. The "Establishment" may be understood as a system of laws through which one's experiences of life are filtered. One must be redeemed from this through the doctrine of love. From Christ's words, we have learned that we should love our neighbors. We are not—as in previous times—to hate our enemies, but to love them instead. Christ also said that man is not made for the Sabbath, but that the Sabbath is made for man. In other words, the Law is to serve man and not man the Law. This represents an enormous transformation of our spiritual understanding of our relationship to each other, God, and laws fashioned by other men in His Name.

Let me remind you of that moment in which Christ transcended all the laws. It is the story of His forty days in the desert. In this case, the Devil represented the Law that had to be transcended. The very first question the Devil put to Christ was, "Why don't you turn these stones into bread?" Christ replies that man lives not by bread alone but by every word that comes from the mouth of God. He rejects the economic theory of the spiritual life, thereby refuting Bernard Shaw's notion that one must be economically well-off before one can practice spiritual exercises.

In the second temptation, the Devil takes Christ up onto the mountain top, showing and offering to Him the lands of the world if He will bow down to him. And Christ says, "Get thee behind me, Satan," thereby transcending the seduction of political power as life's aim.

The Devil then takes Him up to the pinnacle of the temple, suggesting that if Christ is so spiritual, He can cast himself down and God will bear Him up. Christ rejects this temptation to spiritual inflation by saying, "You shall not tempt the Lord thy God." Christ returns then from the desert to preach to the people the new message of the spirit, the message of love.

QUESTION: Does this apply to us? Are we "heroes" on a spiritual journey?

In the European Middle Ages the theme of the individual on an individual quest clearly emerges. This is the theme of the Grail legends. Why should anyone go questing for the Grail in Gothic Europe when the Holy Sacrifice of the Mass was being celebrated in every church? The reason was that the Holy Sacrifice of the Mass was a general sacrament that did not depend on the recipient's or the priest's personal character for its effect. It was a miraculous, magically working conduit of the grace of the Crucifixion of Christ which pours into those who received it. All one had to do was abide by the laws of the Church and examine one's conscience and resolve not to sin again. It was not in itself, however, a test of character.

This mythological Grail was not inside any Church and only the person who had a certain character could find it. The Grail was carried by absolutely virtuous maidens and it represented an integrity of character and life rather than a sacramental system.

Sir Gawain, Arthur's nephew, proposes a vow, that, since they thought it a disgrace to go forth in a group, each should enter the forest at that point where he found it darkest, and where no other path existed. This is the absolute opposite to the Oriental guru system, in which you accept the direction of a guru who knows what is best for you. But it is you and your potential character, which has never been seen and which can be brought into being by no one else, that is the life quest in the Western sense. Each individual pursues it in his or her own way. The problem in our society and in our schools is to inculcate, without overdoing it, the notion of education, as in the Latin *educere*—to lead, to bring out what is in someone rather than merely to indoctrinate him/her from the outside. Spiritually, then, we must all seek the Grail by entering that part of the forest where nobody else has cut a path for us.

QUESTION: Rebirth seems a recurring theme. Can you explain more about its symbolism?

The imagery of rebirth is of two main orders. The moon which dies and is resurrected is the chief symbol of this miracle of rebirth in time. The moon sheds its shadow as the serpent sheds its skin. The serpent also plays a role as the symbol of this same principle of the life that is reborn from its own death. In traditional mythologies, the sacrificial bull, too, is associated with this symbolism of death and rebirth. The horns of the moon are rendered in the horns of the bull. The sacrifice of the bull is symbolic of the sacrifice of that mortal part in us which leads to the release of the eternal.

The sun is our second symbol of rebirth, evoking that idea of not coming back at all, of not being reborn here but of passing beyond the spheres of rebirth altogether to a transcendent light. The typical image for this is the sun. The moon carries darkness within it but wherever the sun goes there is no darkness. There are only the shadows of those forces that do not open themselves to its light. The image of the sun-door speaks of yet another kind of rebirth, that of the return of the lost one—that is, the one who is lost in the spheres of shadows and time, who returns to that eternal root which is his own great root.

As the bull is symbolic of the moon, so the lion, with his great radiant solar face, is the symbolic animal of the sun. As the rising sun quenches the moon and the stars, so the lion's roar scatters the grazing animals, just as the lion's pouncing on the bull symbolizes the sun's extinguishing the moon. If we recall the serpent, we recognize the eagle, the solar bird, as its counterpoint. So we have these parallels: eagle against serpent, lion against bull, sun against moon.

When you realize that eternity is right here now, that it is within your possibility to experience the eternity of your own truth and being, then you grasp the following: That which you are was never born and will never die; that is the insight rendered in terms of the solar mystery, the solar light.

In contrast to ours, the whole aim of Oriental religions is to bring about in us an experience of our identity with that void which is no-void. The goal of these religions is to bring about a realization of this your identity with that which flows to you as experience.

To set the normal position in the West against this, we say God created the world and God and the world are not the same, Creator and creature are not the same, so our religions do not strive for the experience of identity. Our religions intend the rendition of a relationship of that which is not God to God achieved through participation in what is taken to be God's society, or the founded church. In the Hebrew tradition, God has a covenant with a certain people and the relationship to God is through membership in that group. In the Christian tradition, Christ is true God and true Man, which is regarded as a mystery at the center of the Church's claims.

QUESTION: You speak often of the shadows in time as in the symbolism of the moon. Is this the same as suffering in the midst of life?

Gottfried von Strassburg opens his wonderful work *Tristan,* composed about 1210, by saying that suffering and bliss are intrinsic to life and that you cannot have the two separated from one another. "I undertake a labor," he wrote, "out of love for the world and to comfort noble hearts." He addresses the world of "those I love, not for those who as I am told ask only for bliss, life, and joy without pain but those who in their noble hearts sustain bitterness with sweetness, the sweetness of their bitter lives and the bitterness of their sweet lives, and their sweet death." Gottfried goes on to illustrate this theme with the image of Christ crucified, in which the pain of love is rendered as God in His love coming to endure the pain of communication with the beloved, which is to say, Mankind.

This theme was again rendered in those wonderful fourteenth-century German pictures of the Annunciation, in which the Virgin is kneeling in prayer and from a window there comes a beam on which the Christ child comes down to her already carrying his cross. This tells us that love for life includes a willing acquiescence in the pain of life for which the pain and agony themselves, and all that goes with them, are no refutation whatsoever.

The mysticism of battle is a great theme throughout the world's literature. The battlefield is symbolic of the field of life in which all creatures survive because of the deaths of others. Thus we grasp the giving of oneself for whatever it is that is experienced as the object or value of one's love, the great example of which is Christ on the Cross. Schopenhauer says that in this we witness the revelation of the transcendence of the individual. This is the atonement, or at-one-ment, with the Father, the very same father and son motif of which Joyce writes. That mythological motif of the atonement with the father, which has come down through the Christian tradition and been read chiefly in historical terms, is given the sense of an actual experience that anyone of us may have and must have if we are to break past ourselves. It comes, however, in and through a personal relationship, for only in relationship to another can this experience, with its human costs, occur.

It is in human relationships that the operation takes place—the relationship of me to you, of you to another, of you to your job, of you to Earth—relationship is the field where the individual is in process. In marriage, for example, when one sacrifices, one is not sacrificing to the other, one sacrifices rather to the relationship. In the relationship both participate, so you are sacrificing to an aspect of yourself in relation to another, and there is no psychological development outside the relationship. That is what we have in the center. It is the form of a cross. Relationship and yielding. Dark and light together.

I've been happily married forty-eight years, and I ought to know something about it. The important thing in marriage is the relationship between two people, and when one becomes married—I mean *really* has become married—one has shifted the center of regard from oneself to the relationship of the two. And when you think of yourself as sacrificing or giving up things, it is not for the other person that you are doing it, it is for the relationship. And you are as much in the relationship as the other one is, do you see what I mean? This is what you are dealing with, the two together. And you have to think of yourself not as this one, but as these two as one. And I say if your marriage isn't the highest priority in your whole life, you're not married, that's all. And the thing I frequently say is that marriage is not a long love affair.

Now this is the big problem in modern marriage, the idea—it was first announced, as far as I know, in the thirteenth century by Wolfram von Eschenbach—of love as the ground for marriage. Formerly, and in most parts of the world, the society tells you who is going to marry whom through arrangements made by the parents. Love affairs were always dangerous to that idea of marriage. These two ideas of marrying for love-in-marriage that is more than a social convention are brought together in this idea: marriage is the confirmation of love. And love is the sacramentalization of marriage.

Marriage, as I said, is not a love affair; it is an ordeal. If you think of it as that you will be able to go through with it. The ordeal consists specifically in sacrificing ego to the relationship. And ego is always coming up, you know, saying, "Oh, poor me. Nobody's doing my typing for me," and that sort of thing. By the way, I know one great scholar who went through three wives until he got the one that would not only do the typing, but could do it in Greek and Latin as well.

QUESTION: How does the ordinary person achieve transcendence and what role does ritual play in it?

In the dictionary, the word "transcendence" has two distinct definitions. The proper and obvious meaning of the word is "goes past something," or is outside of something, or beyond something. It transcends; it is beyond. The main question is: what is it beyond? The notion that "God is transcendent" means on one level that God is something that is beyond the world. One can have a fact that is beyond the world fact.

The other interpretation of transcendence is "that which is beyond all conceptualization." You cannot, therefore, have any concept of that which is transcendent because it goes beyond any concept in the human mind. In its basic sense, that which transcends is that which transcends all conceptualization, all naming. It is beyond all names and forms.

How does the ordinary person come to the transcendent? For a start, I would say, study poetry. Learn how to read a poem. You need not have the experience to get the message, or at least some indication of the message. It may come gradually. There are many ways, however, of coming to the transcendent experience.

A significant approach is the way of ritual. A ritual allows us to participate in the enactment of a myth. One prepares internally to move with the image and the transcendent comes through. Often those who are interested in the arts in a discursive, historical, art-historical way, suddenly find that one of the works of art really grabs them and they are literally transformed. Think of what it is with music. At a certain age, a certain kind of music interests you and captures your imagination, your internal self, and you participate in it. Then that drops off and another order of music comes in. Art is talking to what is possible within you.

In speaking of ritual, let us examine the initiations of boys and girls in tribal societies. There is a crucial distinction here as we consider how males and females become adults. When does the girl-child become an adult female? At her first menstruation. And what is the fundamental initiation experience that is put upon her? Typically, she is put in a little hut to sit there for a week or so realizing what has happened. It might be said that life overtakes the female. She becomes a woman and presently she becomes a mother.

If we speak of "The Emergence of the Goddess," we refer really to the "The Emergence of the Heroine." A person is a hero or a heroine when he or she is functioning in the interest of values that are not local to the person but are of some greater force of which the person is a vehicle. The woman becomes a heroine as she becomes a vehicle of a force that brings forth life.

Picture a little Bushman boy being nursed by his mother, weaned very late, a little boy already, but still nursing on his mother. That little boy, unlike the little girl, will never become the life-body himself. He must learn to relate to that. The woman need not learn how to relate to the man because that is not the problem. The problem concerns how the man relates to the woman. She is Life. He is a way of relating to Life.

So what happens with the boy? Nothing ever happens. He must, therefore, be beaten up and converted into a vehicle of social function. The woman is the vehicle of nature in the tribal societies and man is the vehicle of the social order. The adult men take the boys out and they beat them up, they carve up their bodies so that they will not have children's bodies anymore and so they enter the service of the society. If they do not go with it, they are killed and eaten. There is no mercy, but from these rites come civilized human beings ready to serve something greater than themselves.

When Catlin, the wonderful artist, was among the Mandan Indians in the upper Missouri in 1832, he attended many of the initiation ceremonials. The young men had wooden spikes put through the pectoral muscles, and were suspended from the ceiling and beaten around until these spikes pulled out. One of them said, "Women suffer and we must suffer, too."

In Brazil, some tribes refer to the men's rites as the men's menstruation. Through these rites they are turned into vehicles of a force that is bigger than themselves. And they thus enter into service to these societies.

QUESTION: The ritual seems to aim at the group. How does the individual participate?

It has been observed that rituals and rites seem to stress the homogeneous nature of experience. How, then, we might ask, does the individual fit into ritual? Wherever you have a ritual, you have a group reference, with everybody participating in the ritual, thinking and finding themselves as members of the same organism. Such rituals always include a lot of people.

We recall that there are two levels to the Greek ritual world and religious world. One consists of the local cults. Martin Nillson, in one of the great studies of the Greek religions, describes going out to Sparta and Boetia to find the deities and characters that are ordinarily encountered in the literary tradition functioning in the service of the cult tradition.

In Athens, however, during the sixth and seventh centuries there came a literary transformation of these local cults. The classical myths come to us in literature as a secondary mythology of the intellectuals of Athens. It was Pisistrates who founded the annual festivals composed of athletic games, new tragedies and comedies of the great poets, and other competitions. Out of such creative celebrations, our general knowledge of classical mythology comes. These were aimed, of course, at the Athenian citizen, rather than the group as in the old local cults. Eleusis becomes the sanctuary of Athens and the mysteries of Eleusis are associated with the Athenian ideal. Even though they originated long before for other purposes, they came to address an individual rather than a group experience. The group that attends is a group only for a moment. It resembles, in a way, a crowd visiting the Pope together in audience. Every person receives the whole experience but then they break up and go their individual ways.

In our culture, we have done everything to break down the ceremonial rituals and the myths they symbolize and reinforce. We Americans have witnessed a pullback from myths and rituals we hold in common into identifications with racial and class groupings. Persons might well ask about what group they associate themselves with mythologically. They may well discover that it is with some ethnic subgrouping rather than national grouping. This is the result of the weakened state of the shared mythology that unites disparate groups.

A powerful example is that of the Hebrew tradition, which, through the annual ritual of the Seder meal at Passover, recapitulates and reinforces the entire history of the Jews as a people. There are great boons, as in this strong sense of being a people together, in this fulfillment of one of the functions of mythology, that of social identity.

Effective ritual can, in the wrong hands, be highly dangerous. This is well personified in Hitler, who was a genius at employing ritual to develop national consciousness. He was a powerful and charismatic speaker at the center of vast rallies which, as a German once told me, with their music, their lighting, and fluttering banners, almost made him, against his will, raise his hand in the Nazi salute.

In the Catholic Church, the ritual of the Mass, especially when believers could find it celebrated in Latin everywhere in the world, was a powerful symbol of and source of identification with a universal church. So, too, was the eating of fish on Friday, especially since the fish is, in itself, so rich on so many levels in mythological identification with Christ.

In America today the picket line or a similar protest line, is one of the few rituals that retains its effectiveness. It is powerful because members of the group are walking and shouting or chanting a slogan together. Nobody is allowed to cross the picket line, which is a space set aside. That picket line is, in a sense, a sacred place.

QUESTION: Would you enlarge on this idea of "sacred space"?

Sacred space may be defined as any space set aside from secular uses, from a stick around which a circle is drawn in India to a great medieval cathedral, so that it is freed from the world of the pairs of opposites, such as gain and loss in everyday business, so that we may contemplate the unity and mystery revealed in all things. In the great sanctuaries and temples everything is symbolic—that is, ordered to being transparent to transcendence.

The earliest examples of sacred space are found in the caves in southern France and northern Spain, where extraordinary symbolic paintings were made 30,000 years ago. When you enter them, your whole consciousness is transformed, and they seem to constitute your primary environment. The animals on the earth above seem merely to be reflections of this subterranean world.

A sacred space, then, is any area, such as the caves, in which everything is done to transform the environment into a metaphor. You may say that "Sacred Space is everywhere," but you can say that only after you have learned the discipline of sacred space, and appreciated the metaphoric significance of the objects found therein. Examine a six-pointed star, for example, which is the fourth cakra in India as well as the Star of David. At the top we have the symbol of aspiration. The down point signifies the obstacle to that aspiration and the other sides signify the means by which to make the ascent. Thus we have symbolized the means for the transition from the field of duality to that of unity—that is, the way of getting beyond all pairs of opposites.

Take the problem of art and sacred space as it is exemplified in the Middle Ages. The late medieval picture of the city of Rheims shows the cathedral in the center. The cathedral is the temple represented as that opening through which transcendence breaks and the energy, here interpreted as God, as supernatural, pours into the field of time.

When at Chartres, outside of Paris, I realized what the glory of that civilization is. This organization of space embodies a notion of the nature of the universe that does not appear anywhere else in the world.

The architecture of the classical world had its beautiful Doric temples, so composed and small that you can put your mind around them. The outside of the temple was what was important. The inside is an empty room with the image of the tomb within it. In the Gothic, however, it is the inside that is important. Suddenly with the dawn of the new culture and inspiration, a new architecture came into being that was in itself a statement of the experience of mystery—the mystery of space.

The flying buttresses hold up the walls from the outside. The main interest of the cathedral is not how it looks from outside, but how it is experienced on the inside. It creates a holy space, a sacred space that does not refer to anything but mystery. When its construction is successful, there results a perfect balance of thrust and support that is itself a statement of energy and space. What we observe is how architecture can render an experience of mystery, an experience of a mode of being.

Chartres possesses the oldest Gothic sculptures in Europe. You have Christ of the Second Coming in the center, and to His right and left are the images of the Virgin. The figures surrounding the Christ of the Second Coming are interpreted in Christianity as Matthew, Mark, Luke, and John. They are actually signs of the zodiac representing the solstices and the equinoxes at the time 2000 B.C., when the spring equinox fell during the sign of the bull, not of the ram. Thus there are found here the bull, the lion, the scorpion bird, and the water carrier. Christ being born is breaking, as it were, from the belt of Mother Universe. And the space in which He sits is simply a representation of the vulva of Christ's birth. He is being born from the womb of Mother Universe. He is the sustaining child of the universe, He, who is the begetter of the universe as well.

There we also find a depiction of Mary's Assumption into Heaven. This illustrates the problem of the survival of archaic mythic images into the contemporary world. There is, as we have mentioned, no place in our cosmology today for either Mary or Jesus to have gone when they ascended. In the age when this mythology was coined, however, the heavens were just a little bit beyond the planet Saturn. With our present understanding, such images become literally incredible. The same problem attends Elijah, who ascended in a four-horsed fiery chariot up to Heaven. Those images must not be cast aside but rather reinterpreted in terms of their psychological meaning. Images of a contemporary sort must also be discovered to render those meanings.

At the center, in the apse around the altar, is a statue of the Black Madonna with the dark Christ on her knee. I do not understand the idea of the Black Madonna. In the crypt of Chartres there is an ivory madonna that is also black. There is also the Holy Ghost as the dove above her head. It is the bird of Venus. That is a good translation for it speaks of the love of God pouring into the world and begetting the Incarnation, parallel to the incarnation of the dove of Aphrodite, the dove of love.

The wonder of Chartres, of course, reveals itself through the windows. The last time I was at Chartres, I learned that the French had gotten the idea of cleaning the windows, and, as a result, they have taken the patina off, which had built up on the outside, and thereby destroyed the optics, the medium essential to the spiritual use of light. In the eighteenth century, the French did worse things; they actually knocked some of the windows out of Chartres to let light in. But the kind of image translated into its windows is that of the Glory of God whose Triune Face is wiped from our sight by the field of blazing light that you see radiate through.

We must, however, ask about who built this cathedral. The answer is: everybody. There is a beautiful book by Henry Adams called *Mont St. Michel and Chartres*. In it he speaks of the Virgin—for all of these temples and cathedrals are to the Virgin—and of the energy generated by this concept of the Virgin being equivalent to the energy generated in his time by the new mechanical dynamos. That is to say, the Virgin electrifies and animates the whole community.

Well, the whole art is devoted to the rendition of a mythology that coordinates the whole society. The Middle Ages were based on a mythology: the Fall in the Garden of Eden, the Redemption on the Cross, and the delivery of the Grace of the Redemption to Mankind through the sacraments of the church. On this mythology the Christian religion is based. And one can read it in the architecture, statuary, windows, and decoration of the cathedrals, the building of which, like the culture itself, was energized by the Virgin. Chartres, and all great churches, are examples of sacred space.

QUESTION: You have referred in your work to the symbols of spiritual growth in the Kundalini yoga. Could you explain that briefly?

The word *Kundalini* means "the coiled-up one," and it refers to the spiritual energy which is regarded as coiled up on itself in most of us most of the time, at a seat at the bottom of the body, actually, right at the anus. The goal of this yoga is to employ breath control and meditation to uncoil that Kundalini so that it comes up a channel in the spine known as *Sushumnā*. And as it does, it passes through the different organic levels of psychological commitment: the genitals, which are the center of sex; the navel, which is aggression; and the heart, which is the opening of its own capacity for compassion; the throat, which is of ascetic austerity; the mind, which is of the beholding of the image of God. The throat is the verbal center, and is related to the left side of the brain, just as the image center is associated with the right side of the brain.

Until you achieve the level of the heart, you remain in kinetic art, that of possession and submission. Consider the difference between lust and love. It is the difference between the second and fourth centers. Dante beholding Beatrice saw her with the eye of the heart. Acteon beholding the goddess Artemis did so with lust. This young hunter was out with his dogs, and he followed a stream to its source, and there was Artemis, the goddess, bathing naked with her nymphs. He looked at her with the eye not of beholding a goddess, cakra four, but cakra two—that is, with lust. She splashed a bit of water on him and he was turned into a stag, which we might observe was what he was in the first place, and his dogs consumed him.

Any reference below cakra four is dangerous in that it is kinetic, in this sense, either of desire or of loathing. I once spent a weekend with psychoanalysts and my role was to lecture on courtly love. They did not know what that was. And I felt as though I were really in the wrong place, for these learned people were adept at analyzing people who were out of joint. They knew as much about pedagogy and teaching people how to live as a garbage collector would about how to cook a good meal. It struck me that trying to solve the problems of cakra two in terms of cakra two is simply doomed to failure. Lust is not cured by more lust. The solution is to be found in terms of cakra four.

Nor can you solve the problems of cakra three in terms of cakra three. Aggression does not remedy aggression. The only way you can civilize little human animals is by civilizing them. That is to say, by opening their heart cakra. And if they cannot open the heart cakra, you can at least give them a system of civilized rules about how to live, which will help them function as though their heart cakra had opened. When illumination comes, and compassion comes, then you do not need rules to tell you how to act compassionately. You are spontaneously compassionate.

You can't make a bad little animal into a good little animal by treating him as though he were an animal. You have to waken the heart cakra, which is the human sentiment of compassion, and understanding, that of love instead of lust. Among the psychoanalysts were men who said they didn't know what love was, but they did know what fetishism was. That is certainly tunnel vision on the human condition. The human animal is found in the pelvic system, with those three first cakras. But the heart is the beginning of humanity.

QUESTION: Can you explore the notion of the Afterlife?

In many traditions we find heavens and purgatories, both in the plural. This concept is present in all reincarnation systems: Jainism, Buddhism, Hinduism, and in the Persian system as well. The idea centers on persons in what might be called the "eternal sphere," in which their experiences reflect or recapitulate those of their lives in time.

Hell, properly, is the condition of people who are so bound to their ego lives and selfish values that they cannot open out to a transpersonal grace. It is beyond them to open themselves to something that will work as a spiritually transforming influence. They are therefore stuck with what they are, in this stunted phase, for eternity. That is the Christian idea of Hell.

Christianity is the only religion that has the idea of a permanent condition called Hell. A mortal sin is regarded as an offense that condemns a person to Hell. Other religious systems view the Hell idea more as Christians do Purgatory—that is, as a transit of purgation. One dies so bound to a limited system of values that one couldn't possibly open to the transcendence of the Beatific Vision of God in that condition. Purgatory is a pedagogical place and the ranges of Heaven are spread out according to the possibilities of one's spiritual realization.

When I was a little boy, I asked the nun who was my teacher, "If I go to Heaven will I have the same experience as Thomas Aquinas?"

"Well," she said, "Your cup will be full, but it will be a little cup." That was not a bad answer.

APPENDIX

A DISCUSSION

INTRODUCTORY NOTE

In early 1979, Glenn Collins, then an editor of The New York Times Magazine, *asked me to interview Joseph Campbell, whom I had known for several years, for their Easter edition. This gave me the unique opportunity of having an extended question period of my own on the focused subject of the related religious feasts of Passover and Easter. It also allowed an extended discussion of a subject we had often discussed, that of the transformation of our spiritual consciousness in the dawning of the Age of Space.*

We spent a wintry February day in his apartment near Washington Square. The resulting article, which did appear on Easter Sunday under the title "Earthrise—The Dawning of a New Spiritual Awareness," attracted more attention to his work, Campbell later wrote to me, than any previous interview and indeed, brought him to the attention of Bill Moyers for the first time. Those were happy providential outcomes of a meeting that was in itself its own reward. In it Joseph Campbell integrates and expounds on many of the themes found in the lectures of this collection. As such it is not an unfitting conclusion for this volume.

—E.C.K.

EARTHRISE—THE DAWNING OF A
NEW SPIRITUAL AWARENESS

Although the word is popularly used to denote falsehood, myth is actually a perennial vehicle for expressing truth. Human beings have always been told, in mythic forms, the stories they want to be remembered and passed on—such as the Arthurian legends or the enduring biblical tales—to distinguish them from fashions, fads, or the constantly changing facts of almanacs or the *Guinness Book of World Records.* Myth and symbol are fundamental and essential properties of all religions; they are the special language of religious experience.

Joseph Campbell has devoted his life to their study, detecting recurrent themes and motifs in the varied mythologies of different cultures that suggest that a single underground spring of religious experience nourishes them all. According to Campbell, what appear to be diverse religious traditions are actually different expressions of a unitary experience that is shared across all cultures.

The author of numerous books on comparative religion and mythology, and a former professor at Sarah Lawrence College in Bronxville, New York, Campbell is perhaps best known for *The Hero with a Thousand Faces,* published in 1949. In this work he traced the stories of ancient and contemporary heroes, showing that their challenges and experiences were essentially the same, that every man was indeed Everyman. The pattern that could be discerned in the timeless stories and symbols of myth could also be discovered in our own lives. As Campbell once told an interviewer, "The latest incarnation of Oedipus, the continued romance of Beauty and the Beast, stand this afternoon at the corner of Forty-second Street and Fifth Avenue, waiting for the light to change."

Campbell's own life parallels that of the mythic hero's journeys and struggles, as he found both the identity and the path of scholarship that were true for him. A New Yorker of Irish Catholic descent who was captivated by Buffalo Bill's Wild West Show as a boy, he began his studies of American Indian culture and experience. Gradually he awakened to the dream of pervasive mythological themes and was called, as he felt within himself, to a long pilgrimage of discovery that led him not only to his own graduate study of the Arthurian romances at Columbia University, but also to European studies of Oriental philosophy, religion, and Sanskrit as well as the works of Freud and Jung. In all of these he recognized the common themes that were found in the American Indian culture of his boyhood wonder and the Catholic Church of his boyhood belief.

KENNEDY: "Myth" is still a confusing term for many people. Perhaps we could begin by explaining it a little more in detail.

CAMPBELL: Myth has many functions. The first we might term mystical, in that myth makes a connection between our waking consciousness and the whole mystery of the universe. That is its cosmological function. It allows us to see ourselves in relationship to nature, as when we speak of Father Sky and Mother Earth. There is also a sociological function for myth, in that it supports and validates a certain social and moral order for us. The story of the Ten Commandments given to Moses by God on Mount Sinai is an example of this. Lastly, myth has a psychological function, in that it offers us a way of passing through, and dealing with, the various stages from birth to death.

KENNEDY: You have written of the difficulty of one mythological system's being able to speak to a world which has become so varied. The agrarian and hunting myths that once spoke to everyone no longer apply quite so easily. But you have also said that, with some reflection, we can understand that the ancient stories of heroes and their adventures are the same as our contemporary search for meaning.

CAMPBELL: Yes, myths come out of the creative imagination we all share, and the story each of us recognizes in our own search for spiritual meaning parallels all the legends of heroes, like the knights of the Round Table, who must travel to an unknown world and do battle with the powers of darkness in order to return with the gift of knowledge.

KENNEDY: We are, according to many observers, at a turning point in religious consciousness. That is, the mythological structure—or the legends that undergirded a literal biblical interpretation of the universe—are sharply challenged by the discoveries of the Space Age.

CAMPBELL: Yes, that is exactly what is happening, with consequences we can all see. One must remember the central truth, for example, about Easter and Passover. We are all called out of the house of bondage, even as the Jews were called out of their bondage in Egypt. We are called out of bondage in the way in which the moon throws off its shadow to emerge anew, in the way that life throws off the shadow of death. Easter and Passover have the same roots; we are called out of bondage to our old tradition. Easter is not Easter and Passover is not Passover unless they release us even from the tradition that gives us these feasts.

Easter and Passover are prime symbols of what we are faced with in the Space Age. We are challenged both mystically and socially, because our ideas of the universe have been reordered by our experience in space. The consequence is that we can no longer hold on to the religious symbols that we formulated when we thought that the earth was the center of the universe.

KENNEDY: You are saying that the perennial power of myth is that it can shed one formulation—such as the pre-Copernican notion of an Earth down here and Heaven up there—and yet retain and renew its strength. That means that we are experiencing the mythological truth, in the very challenge to give up the religious understanding of the universe that is very strong in Judeo-Christian imagery. And that the Passover-Easter experience demands that we do that.

CAMPBELL: Easter and Passover make us experience in ourselves a call out of bondage, yes, but so experiencing them does not destroy the religious tradition. Understanding these symbols in their transcendent spiritual sense enables us to see and to possess our religious traditions freshly. The space age demands that we change our ideas about ourselves, but we want to hold on to them. That is why there is a resurgence of old-fashioned orthodoxy in so many areas at the present time. There are no horizons in space, and there can be no horizons on our own experience. We cannot hold on to ourselves and our in-groups as we once did. The space age makes that impossible, but people reject this demand or don't want to think about it. So they pull back into one true church, or black power, or the unions, or the capitalist class.

KENNEDY: Then the Space Age challenges everything that makes us earth centered or group centered.

CAMPBELL: Easter and Passover offer the perfect symbols because they mean that we are called to a new life. This new life is not very well defined:

that is why we want to hold on to the past. The journey to this new life—and it is a journey we must all make—cannot be made unless we let go of the past. The reality of living in space means that we are born anew, not born again to an old-time religion but to a new order of things. There are no horizons—that is the meaning of the Space Age. We are in a free fall into a future that is mysterious. It is very fluid and this is disconcerting to many people. All you have to do is know how to use a parachute.

KENNEDY: An awareness of mythological truth alerts us to the fact that in the Easter experience we do not just remember historical events but that we are experiencing in ourselves Passover and Easter, that what we feel is the pull of the space age on our own religious consciousness.

CAMPBELL: Yes, we can feel it in ourselves. The Space Age, which many people want to forget or write off as a bad investment, is central to all this. Almost fifteen years ago we had the great symbol of change that has taken place. Men stood on the moon and looked back and by television we were able to look back with them—to see earthrise. That is the symbol that enabled us to feel the truth of the discovery that Copernicus made four and a quarter centuries ago. Until then, we may have agreed theoretically with Copernicus but his map of the universe was not available to us, except to mathematicians and astronomers. It was an invisible idea and we could go on thinking, as we did, about a religious idea in which everything was divided along the same lines that the heavens and the earth were divided.

KENNEDY: If Heaven and Earth were divided, so too were body and soul, nature and supernature, flesh and spirit. The universe was ordered in a hierarchical fashion and so too were the churches.

CAMPBELL: This divided model allowed us to think that there was a spiritual order, separate or divided from our own experience. Think of how we spoke about things according to that old model. Everything was seen from earthbound eyes. The sun rose and set. Joshua stopped both the sun and the moon to have time to finish a slaughter.

With the moon walk, the religious myth that sustained these notions could no longer be held. With our view of earthrise, we could see that the earth and the heavens were no longer divided but that the earth is in the heavens. There is no division and all the theological notions based on the distinction between the heavens and the earth collapse with that realization. There is a unity in the universe and a unity in our own experience. We can no longer look for a spiritual order outside of our own experience.

KENNEDY: That challenges the old ideas that our fate is being decided "out there" by the gods.

CAMPBELL: Or that the stars are their residences, hung with their lanterns. You can still see remnants of that in the disappointment many people feel when our scientific probes do not discover life on Mars.

KENNEDY: Isn't it true that Carl Jung once said that the declaration of the Assumption of the Virgin Mary by the Roman Catholic Church was the most significant religious declaration of the century? Is this a place where we can see the interlocking of literal and symbolic levels of religious statements?

CAMPBELL: Jung did say that and, of course, he was pointing to the profound symbolic, rather than literal, meaning of that doctrine. Literally, it suggests a heaven "up there" to which a body could ascend. But that is a religious doctrine based on a divided notion of the universe. Symbolically, the same tradition suggests it signifies the return of Mother Earth to the heavens, the very thing that has occurred because of our journeys into space.

KENNEDY: Earthrise is a symbol that is working its way slowly into our consciousness. One sees it in many places. CBS News used it for a long time on their evening news. Strangely enough, it has been used—set afire, however—to publicize the movie *The Late Great Planet Earth*. That is a fire-and-brimstone account of the end of the world in literal biblical terms. That use of earthrise seems a good example of the resistance you describe to the space age and its central metaphor.

CAMPBELL: The sense of the apocalypse is very widespread and I believe it is a rejection of this new age. That is why there is so much interest in disaster. It's more than just the thrill of the movies. It is evidence of how deep the notion of the apocalyptic moment is. We hate ourselves so much that we take delight in the destruction of people. It is like reading the worst of the prophets in the Bible.

The coming of the second millennium may be accentuating this. We can really expect some of the same things that attended the approach of the year 1000 to occur again. It is in everyone's mind at some level.

We must not understand apocalypse literally, not as some physical destruction and judgment on the world, or as something that is going to occur in the future. The kingdom is here; it does not come through expectation. One looks at the world and sees the radiance. The Easter revelation is right there. We don't have to wait for something to happen. So, in the space age, two themes are evident. First, we must move socially into a new system of symbols, because the old ones do not work. Second, the symbols, as they exist, when they are interpreted spiritually rather than concretely, yield the revelation.

The mystical theme of the space age is this: the world, as we know it, is coming to an end. The world as the center of the universe, the world divided from the heavens, the world bound by horizons in which love is reserved for members of the in-group: that is the world that is passing away. Apocalypse does not point to a fiery Armageddon but to the fact that our ignorance and our complacency are coming to an end. Our divided, schizophrenic worldview, with no mythology adequate to coordinate our conscious and unconscious—that is what is coming to an end. The exclusivism of there being only one way in which we can be saved, the idea that there is a single religious group that is in sole possession of the truth—that is the world as we know it that must pass away. What is the kingdom? It lies in our realization of the ubiquity of the divine presence in our neighbors, in our enemies, in all of us.

KENNEDY: Much, then, of what we recognize as retrenchment in various religious traditions is a rejection of facing the Easter-Passover demands of passing into the space age?

CAMPBELL: The central demand is to surrender our exclusivity, everything that defines us over against each other. People have used religious affiliations to do this for years. There are two pages in Martin Buber that almost merit his reputation. He speaks of the "I-Thou" and the "I-It" relationships. An ego talking to a thou is different from an ego talking to an it. Whenever we emphasize otherness or out-groups, we are making persons into "it." The Gentile, the Jew, the enemy—they all become the same.

KENNEDY: What about ethnicity and the emphasis on the search for roots that are so popular these days?

CAMPBELL: It is understandable that people want to search out their roots, especially after all the dislocation and emigration of the last century. Still, an overemphasis on this, understandable though it may be, is a sign of pulling back into in-groups. That is why we see so many movements that are intensely nationalistic or, in recent years in Iran, one that is almost xenophobic, a wish to turn the clock back a thousand years and to reject relationship with any out-group. But our actual ultimate tool is in our common humanity, not in our personal genealogy.

KENNEDY: The notion of taking one world seriously, despite the awareness we have developed through studying ecology, is still very frightening.

CAMPBELL: It means we have to give up what we know, what we are comfortable with. People draw back to what seems more familiar ground to them.

KENNEDY: Is there an explanation here for the fascination with deliverance from powers coming from "out there," whether it is Superman coming from Krypton, or visitors in various spacecraft?

CAMPBELL: It is a clear reflection of an outmoded understanding of the universe, that we will be delivered by some benign visitation, by forces from other planets. It is the idea of the kingdom's coming from a source other than from within ourselves. The Kingdom of God is within us but we have this idea that the gods act from "out there."

KENNEDY: Is that where we get the impression of unidentified flying objects?

CAMPBELL: It is part of the same thing. As Jung once wrote, unidentified flying objects tell us something of mankind's visionary expectations. People are looking for visits from the outside world. They think our deliverance will come from there, whereas the Space Age reminds us that it must come from within ourselves. The voyages into outer space turn us back to inner space.

KENNEDY: Then films such as *Close Encounters of the Third Kind* are really old-fashioned stories. They don't really tell us about the future.

CAMPBELL: Such a movie is about the past, not the future. It is the idea that we will be visited by friendly forms, that they will come to our aid and save us.

KENNEDY: Still, the fact that so many creative persons, so many modern mythmakers, are trying to deal with the impact of space explorations tells us that they feel something in their bones about this change. Do any of these movies capture a sense of what we are talking about?

CAMPBELL: I thought that *2001: A Space Odyssey* was very interesting in the way in which it dealt with symbols. You recall, at the beginning, that we see a community of little manlike apes, australopithecines, snarling and fighting with each other. But there is one among them who is different, one who is drawn out of curiosity to approach and explore, one who has a sense of awe before the unknown. This one is apart and alone, seated in wonder before a panel of stone standing mysteriously upright in the landscape. He contemplates it, then he reaches out and touches it cautiously, somewhat in the way the first astronaut's foot approached and then gently touched down on the moon. Awe, you see, is what moves us forward. That's what the filmmaker recognized, that there was a continuity through all time of this motivating principle in the evolution of our species. So the panel is seen later on the moon approached by astronauts. And again, floating in space, mysterious still.

KENNEDY: The point is not to argue over the literal symbolism of the slabs but to let them speak to us as symbols. This is what you mean by religious symbols.

CAMPBELL: Yes, they do not represent historical facts. A symbol doesn't just point to something else. As Thomas Merton wrote, a symbol contains a structure that awakens our consciousness to a new awareness of the inner meaning of life and reality itself. Through symbols we enter emotionally into contact with our deepest selves, with each other, and with God—a word that is to be understood as a symbol. When theologians spoke of God's being dead, a decade or so ago, just as the space age began, they were really saying that their symbols were dead.

KENNEDY: You see a distinction between religion based on the literal interpretation of symbols as historical events and one in which the symbols are mystical references that help us see into ourselves.

CAMPBELL: Yes, the latter is the religion of mysticism, the other a religion of belief in concrete objects, God as a concrete object. In order to understand a concrete symbol we have to let go of it. When you can let the literal meaning of a religious tradition die, then it comes alive again. And this also frees you to respect other religious traditions more. You don't have to be afraid of losing something when you let go of your tradition.

KENNEDY: Isn't something like this actually happening in some religious bodies? In the Roman Catholic Church, for example, many people no longer readily accept the authority of the clergy to regulate their lives, but at the same time they discover they are close to and even like their Catholic tradition. They seem to possess it in a new way.

CAMPBELL: Yes, that is happening in many groups. Many people have learned to let religious symbols speak directly to themselves to order their lives. They don't believe that a group of bishops or other religious leaders could meet in conference and decide for them which interpretation of a symbol must be believed. But they don't reject their religious tradition. They discover that symbols, when they are not pressed literally, can speak clearly across different traditions. The churches have to ask themselves: Are we going to emphasize the historical Christ, or the second person of the Blessed Trinity, the one who knows the Father? If you emphasize the historical, you deemphasize the spiritual power that is the symbol of the basic consciousness that is within us.

KENNEDY: Isn't it disconcerting for a person to reexamine his or her own religious tradition that way?

CAMPBELL: Yes, that is the problem of letting the tradition die. The mystical writer Meister Eckhart once wrote that the ultimate leave-taking is the leaving of God for God. People feel panicky at the thought that we might all have something in common, that they are giving up some exclusive hold on the truth. It is something like discovering that you are a Frenchman and a human being at the same time. That is exactly the challenge that the great religions face in the Space Age.

KENNEDY: So, in this freefall into the future, understanding our religious symbols is a way of using our parachutes. What about symbols of religious worship?

CAMPBELL: Well, they are meant to be respected, but often they are not. Preachers think they have to explain them instead of letting them speak for themselves. That is why the destruction of the Catholic liturgy in the name of reform was such a disaster. It was an effort to make ancient symbols and rituals more rational. And they threw out the Gregorian chant and other great symbolic achievements in the process; they disowned religious symbols that spoke directly to people without need of mediation. The old ritual of the mass spoke powerfully to people. Now the celebrant carries out a Julia Child sort of function at the altar.

KENNEDY: The justification was that it was the reasonable thing to do. But worship is not reasonable in that sense. You have written that part of our loss of a sense of meaning, our "Waste Land" experience, is due to the fact that we have lost our connections with a mystical understanding of our lives.

CAMPBELL: The problem has been that institutionalized religions have not allowed symbols to speak directly to people in their proper sense. Religious traditions translate mythological signs into references to historical events, whereas properly they stem from the human imagination and speak back to the psyche. Historical events are given spiritual meaning by being interpreted mythologically, for instance, with virgin births, resurrections, and miraculous passages of the Red Sea. When you translate the Bible with excessive literalism, you demythologize it. The possibility of a convincing reference to the individual's own spiritual experience is lost.

KENNEDY: How would you define mythology here?

CAMPBELL: My favorite definition of mythology: other people's religion. My favorite definition of religion: misunderstanding of mythology. The misunderstanding consists in the reading of the spiritual mythological symbols as though they were primarily references to historical events. Localized provincial readings separate the various religious communities. Remythologization—recapturing the mythological meaning—reveals a common spirituality of mankind. At Easter, to return to our example, we might suggest the renewal of the knowledge of our general spiritual life through casting off, for a moment, our various historical connections.

KENNEDY: Remythologization would rescue the stories of the Bible, then, from historical literalism and a susceptibility to debunking. Can we connect that with the example of the Easter experience? What of the Cross and the Crucifixion?

CAMPBELL: If we think of the Crucifixion only in historical terms we lose the reference of the symbol immediately to ourselves. Jesus left his mortal body on the cross, the sign of the earth, to go to the Father with whom he was one. We, similarly, are to identify with the eternal life that is within us. The symbol at the same time tells us of God's willing acceptance of the cross—that is to say, participation in the trials and sorrows of human life in the world. So that He is here within us—not by way of a fall or a mistake, but with rapture and joy. Thus the cross has a dual sense—one, our going to the divine, and the other, the coming of the divine to us. It is a true crossing.

KENNEDY: What about the symbols of Easter and Passover? How would one, as you have said, let go of these in order to possess them anew in this first generation of the Space Age?

CAMPBELL: What has always been basic to resurrection, or Easter, is crucifixion. If you want to resurrect, you must have crucifixion. Too many interpretations of the Crucifixion have failed to emphasize that. They emphasize the calamity of the event. And if you emphasize calamity, then you look for someone to blame. That is why people have blamed the Jews for it. But it is not a calamity if it leads to new life. Through the Crucifixion we were unshelled, we were able to be born to resurrection. That is not a calamity. We must look freshly at this so that its symbolism can be sensed.

St. Augustine speaks of going to the cross as a bridegroom to his bride. There is an affirmation here. In the Prado there is a great painting by Titian of Simon of Cyrene as he willingly helps Jesus with the cross. The picture captures the human participation, the free, voluntary participation we all must have in the Easter-Passover mystery.

KENNEDY: So one must step out of one's tradition to see it clearly again.

CAMPBELL: That is what we are challenged to do. Self-preservation is only the second law of life. The first law is that you and the other are one. Politicians love to talk about "I worship in my way, and he in his." But that doesn't make sense if we are one with each other. That is the truth the Space Age urges on us, but many religious institutions resist it.

KENNEDY: Perhaps we can explore the Easter-Passover symbolism in more detail. These feasts, calculated according to the full moon, share much in common.

CAMPBELL: Here we face very similar themes in the Jewish and Christian traditions. The theme is also found in the mystery religions in which Adonis dies and is resurrected.

KENNEDY: And all these come at springtime, matching the bursting forth of flowers and the return of the sun. Even the plangent longing we experience at this season must be related to this.

CAMPBELL: Yes, it is very much the longing to be born anew the way nature is. All these elements fit together. Easter is calculated as the Sunday that follows the first full moon after the vernal equinox. It is evidence of a concern centuries before Christ to coordinate the lunar and solar calendars. What we have to recognize is that these celestial bodies represented to the ancients two different modes of eternal life, one engaged in the field of time, like throwing off death, as the moon its shadow, to be born again; the other, disengaged and eternal. The dating of Easter according to both lunar and solar calendars suggests that life, like the light that is reborn in the moon and eternal in the sun, finally is one.

KENNEDY: What of some of the folk symbols of Easter and Passover? Do they all have similar lunar and solar resonations?

CAMPBELL: There is, to begin with, the rabbit, the Easter bunny. Many peoples of the world see a rabbit in the shadows of the moon. The rabbit is associated with the dying and the resurrection of the moon. The egg is shelled off by the chick as the shadow of the moon is by the moon reborn, or as slough by the birth of the spirit at Easter.

Birds in flight are symbolic of the spirit released from the bondage of earth. So the moon rabbit, the cast-off eggshell, and the just-born bird that is to fly give us together a playful, childlike reading of the Easter message.

———◈◈◈———

It has drawn on in the day as Campbell, with the broad grin of an Irish cop, returns to his reflections about space. The walls of the apartment seem to slide away like a roof of a planetarium and he stands, a boy from the sidewalks of New York who watched Glenn Curtiss's first wobbly plane flight above Riverside Drive more than seventy years ago, Merlin standing with a pointer at the gates of the cosmos.

CAMPBELL: The problem is that people have tried to look away from space and from the meaning of the moon landing. I remember seeing a picture of an astronaut standing on the moon. It was up at Yale and someone had scrawled on it, "So what?" That is the arrogance of the kind of academic narrowness one too often sees; it is trapped in its own predictable prejudices, its own stale categories. It is the mind dulled to the poetry of existence. It's fashionable now to demand some economic payoff from space, some reward to prove it was all worthwhile. Those who say this resemble the apelike creatures in *2001*. They are fighting for food among themselves, while one separates himself from them and moves to the slab, motivated by awe. That is the point they are missing. He is the one who evolves into a human being; he is the one who understands the future.

There have been budget cuts in the space program. We shrug it off, but that is where we live. It is not "out there." And the great symbol remains, that remarkable view of earthrise. Earthrise is like all symbols. They resemble compasses. One point is in a fixed place but the other moves to the unknown. The fear of the unknown, this freefall into the future, can be detected all around us. But we live in the stars and we are finally moved by awe to our greatest adventures. The Kingdom of God is within us. Easter and Passover, particularly, remind us that we have to let go in order to enter it.

CHAPTER NOTES

INTRODUCTION

1   "On the Foundations of Morality," *Sämtliche Werke,* Arthur Schopenhauer (Verlag der Cotta'schen Buchhandlung, 1895–1898), p. 293.

2   *Ibid.*

3   *Op. cit.,* p. 254.

4   *Op. cit.,* p. 293.

5   *The Inner Reaches of Outer Space: Metaphor as Myth and as Religion,* Joseph Campbell (Alfred van der Mark Editions, 1986), p. 113.

6   "Campbell and Catholicism," *Common Boundary,* March/April 1992, Pythia Peay, pp. 28–33.

CHAPTER I

This material on the meaning and function of myth is drawn from Joseph Campbell's lectures entitled "Metaphor as Myth and as Religion" presented at the Jung Institute in San Francisco (tapes L916, L917, L918 in the Joseph Campbell Foundation's audio archives), in 1985. These were augmented from the notes of the editor (Eugene Kennedy) from an interview with Campbell on March 4, 1986, in Honolulu, and later published in the

Forum section of the *National Catholic Reporter*. The occasion of the interview was the forthcoming publication of *The Inner Reaches of Outer Space: Metaphor as Myth and as Religion,* in which a fuller treatment of this and related subjects may be found.

The material on metaphor as the native tongue of myth is drawn from four lectures presented at the University of Beloit, Beloit, Wisconsin, in January 1969.

7   *Historical Atlas of World Mythology, Volume I: The Way of the Animal Powers,* Joseph Campbell (Alfred van der Marck Editions, 1983).

CHAPTER 2

This material has been drawn from lectures delivered by Campbell entitled "Symbolism and Mystical Experience" (tapes L117, L121, L122, L124, L126, L127) presented at Wainwright House between October 3 and December 12, 1966.

Other material has been taken from lectures on "Mystical Experience and the Hero's Journey," given at the Esalen Institute in Big Sur, California (tapes L179, L180), on October 13 and October 14, 1967. Some material was incorporated from his "Way of Contemplation," given on October 15, 1967, at the same institute. A few quotations have also been added from Campbell's participation in a panel discussion, "What Is Spirituality?" (tape L835) recorded on October 10, 1983, at Esalen. A small amount of material is taken from "The Need and Importance of Rites" (tape L90), a lecture delivered by Campbell at the Cooper Union in New York City on January 20, 1964. For a fuller exposition of this theme, cf. *Myths to Live By* (New York, Arkana, 1993).

For a fuller treatment of the hero themes, cf. *The Hero with a Thousand Faces* (Princeton, New Jersey, Princeton University Press, Bollingen Series, second edition, 1968).

Cf. also Campbell's extended treatment of "The Metaphysical-Mystical Prospect," p. 609 ff., in *The Masks of God: Creative Mythology* (New York, The Viking Press, Viking Compass Edition, 1970). Campbell's references to Wittgenstein on the mystical (Op. cit., p. 675) are particularly relevant for those interested in the both the sources and the breadth of Campbell's intellectual inquiry. The Christian mystical tradition is discussed at length (p. 588 ff.) in the section on "The New Universe."

8   *My View of the World,* Erwin Schrödinger (Cambridge University Press, 1964), p. 22.

CHAPTER 3

Some of this chapter is based on "Metaphor as Myth and as Religion" (tape L918) presented at the Jung Institute, San Francisco, 1985. Additional material was taken from a series of lectures entitled, "The Experience of Mystery" presented at the Theatre of the Open Eye, in New York City on April 23 and April 24, 1983.

Most of this chapter is based on *Man and Myth: Imagination and Its Relation to Theological Enquiry,* ed. Malcolm Spicer, Department of Theological Studies, Loyola of Montreal (Editions Declee & Cie., 1973).

9   A fuller discussion of the Kantian concept of the a priori forms of sensibility and the philosophy of *māyā* may be found in *The Masks of God: Oriental Mythology* (Viking Press, 1962), pp. 13f., 177, 184, 237, 254, 335–336.

10 Cf. *The Inner Reaches of Outer Space* for a fuller exploration of this idea.

11 For an extended discussion of the origin of the Gospel of Thomas, cf. *The Masks of God: Occidental Mythology* (Viking Press, 1964), p. 363.

12 "The Waste Land," *Collected Poems 1909–1962,* T.S. Eliot (Harcourt Brace and World, 1963).

13 *Meister Eckhart,* Franz Pfeiffer, trans. C. de B. Evans, 2 vols. (John W. Watkins, 1947), sermon 98.

CHAPTER 4

A portion of this chapter derives from the lecture "Metaphor as Myth and as Religion" (tape L918) presented at the Jung Institute, San Francisco, in 1985.

This chapter is also rooted in sections of *Man and Myth: Imagination and Its Relation to Theological Enquiry,* cited above. This was in turn based on the lecture, "Imagination and Its Relation to Theological Enquiry," presented at Loyola University, Montreal, Canada, on October 17, 1972.

14 *A Portrait of the Artist as a Young Man,* James Joyce (Jonathan Cape, Ltd., 1916. Viking Compass Edition, 1964), pp. 232–233.

15 This is Pope Boniface VIII's dogma, stated in his bull, Unam Sanctam ("single holiness"). It translates, "No salvation outside the Church!"

CHAPTER 5

Much of this chapter is conflated from two lectures with the same theme, both entitled "Genesis and Exodus as History and Myth." The first was given at Hillel Jewish Center in Los Angeles, California, on October 17, 1985 (tape L858). The second was given at the Theatre of the Open Eye, New York City, on December 10, 1985 (2 tapes, L859).

Fuller treatments of some of these themes, in a slightly different context, may be found in Campbell's *The Masks of God: Creative Mythology* (Viking Press, Compass Edition, 1970), as, for example, in the third chapter, "The Word Behind Words," pp. 83–171.

16 "Die Daten der Genesis," Königliche Gesellschaft der Wissenschaften zu Göttingen, Nachrichten 10, Julius (Jules) Oppert (1877), pp. 201–27. Cf. also "The Mystery Number of the Goddess," *The Mythic Dimension,* Joseph Campbell (1993) for a fuller exploration of the numerology of the spirit and of the dual nature of the narrative in Genesis.

CHAPTER 6

A large part of this chapter is taken from "Archetypes of the Christ Legend" (L337), lectures at the Mann Ranch Seminar on April 3, 1971. Other material derives from the lecture, "Symbols of the Christian Faith" (L407), given at the Blaisdell Institute in Claremont, California, in April 1972. Further sections of this chapter were taken from "The Vocabulary of the Christian Faith: When Terms Have Lost Their Mythic Power," given at Trinity Presbyterian Church, Atlanta, Georgia, on May 31, 1971.

Some of the material on the symbolism of the cross is based on Campbell's article, "The Interpretation of Symbolic Forms" from *The Binding of Proteus: Perspectives on Myth and the Literary Process,* edited by

Marjorie W. McCune, Tucker Orbison, and Philip M. Withim (Bucknell University Press, 1980.)

Further treatments of some of these themes may be found in *The Masks of God: Occidental Mythology* (Viking Press, Compass Edition, 1970).

Biblical names were checked in and interpolated brief descriptions are based on *Dictionary of the Bible,* John L. McKenzie (Macmillan Publishing Company, 1965).

17 *Joseph and his Brothers,* Thomas Mann, trans. H. T. Lowe-Porter (Alfred Knopf, 1934).
18 Hávamál 139–142, *The Poetic Edda,* translated by Henry Adams Bellows (American-Scandinavian Foundation, Oxford University Press, 1923), pp. 60–61.

Chapter 7

These questions and answers are edited versions of actual question sessions following the lectures listed above.

Chapter 8

This chapter is taken from an article by the editor, Eugene Kennedy, published in *The New York Times Magazine* on April 15, 1979. This article was in turn based on an interview conducted with Campbell in New York City on February 8, 1979.

A JOSEPH CAMPBELL BIBLIOGRAPHY

Following are the major books authored and edited by Joseph Campbell. Each entry gives bibliographic data concerning the first edition. For information concerning all other editions, please refer to the mediagraphy on the Joseph Campbell Foundation website (www.jcf.org).

AUTHOR

Where the Two Came to their Father: A Navaho War Ceremonial Given by Jeff King. Bollingen Series I. With Maud Oakes and Jeff King. Richmond, Virginia: Old Dominion Foundation, 1943.

A Skeleton Key to Finnegans Wake. With Henry Morton Robinson. New York: Harcourt, Brace & Co., 1944.

The Hero with a Thousand Faces. Bollingen Series XVII. New York: Pantheon Books, 1949.

The Flight of the Wild Gander: Explorations in the Mythological Dimension. New York: Viking Press, 1969. *

The Masks of God, 4 vols. New York: Viking Press, 1959–1968. Vol. 1, *Primitive Mythology,* 1959. Vol. 2, *Oriental Mythology,* 1962. Vol. 3, *Occidental Mythology,* 1964. Vol. 4, *Creative Mythology,* 1968.

Myths to Live by. New York, Viking Press, 1972.

The Mythic Image. Bollingen Series C. Princeton: Princeton University Press, 1974.

Inner Reaches of Outer Space: Metaphor as Myth and as Religion. New York: Alfred van der Marck Editions, 1986. *

The Historical Atlas of World Mythology:

Vol. 1, *The Way of the Animal Powers.* New York: Alfred van der Marck Editions, 1983. Reprint in 2 pts. Part 1, *Mythologies of the Primitive Hunters and Gatherers.* New York: Alfred van der Marck Editions, 1988. Part 2, *Mythologies of the Great Hunt.* New York: Alfred van der Marck Editions, 1988.

Vol. 2, *The Way of the Seeded Earth,* 3 pts. Part 1, *The Sacrifice.* New York: Alfred van der Marck Editions, 1988. Part 2, *Mythologies of the Primitive Planters: The North Americas.* New York: Harper & Row Perennial Library, 1989. Part 3, *Mythologies of the Primitive Planters: The Middle and Southern Americas.* New York: Harper & Row Perennial Library, 1989.

The Power of Myth with Bill Moyers. With Bill Moyers. Ed. Betty Sue Flowers. New York: Doubleday, 1988.

Transformations of Myth through Time. New York: Harper and Row, 1990.

The Hero's Journey: Joseph Campbell on His Life and Work. Ed. Phil Cousineau. New York: Harper and Row, 1990.

Reflections on the Art of Living: A Joseph Campbell Companion. Ed. Diane K. Osbon. New York: HarperCollins, 1991.

Mythic Worlds, Modern Worlds: On the Art of James Joyce. Ed. Edmund L. Epstein. New York: HarperCollins, 1993.

Baksheesh and Brahman: Indian Journal 1954–1955. Eds. Robin and Stephen Larsen and Antony Van Couvering. New York: HarperCollins, 1995.

The Mythic Dimension: Selected Essays 1959–1987. Ed. Antony Van Couvering. New York: HarperCollins, 1997.

Thou Art That. Ed. Eugene Kennedy. Novato, California: New World Library, 2001. *

---

* Published by New World Library as part of the Collected Works of Joseph Campbell.

EDITOR

Books Edited and Completed from the Posthuma of Heinrich Zimmer:

Myths and Symbols in Indian Art and Civilization. Bollingen Series VI. New York: Pantheon, 1946.

The King and the Corpse. Bollingen Series XI. New York: Pantheon, 1948.

Philosophies of India. Bollingen Series XXVI. New York: Pantheon, 1951.

The Art of Indian Asia. Bollingen Series XXXIX, 2 vols. New York: Pantheon, 1955.

The Portable Arabian Nights. New York: Viking Press, 1951.

Papers from the Eranos Yearbooks. Bollingen Series XXX, 6 vols. Edited with R. F. C. Hull and Olga Froebe-Kapteyn, translated by Ralph Manheim. Princeton: Princeton University Press, 1954–1969.

Myth, Dreams and Religion: Eleven Visions of Connection. New York: E. P. Dutton, 1970.

The Portable Jung. By C. G. Jung. Translated by R. F. C. Hull. New York: Viking Press, 1971.

My Life and Lives. By Rato Khyongla Nawang Losang. New York: E. P. Dutton, 1977.

INDEX

A

Abelard, 22
Abraham, 53–60
Adam and Eve, 42, 76, 81. *See also*
    Fall; Garden of Eden; Genesis
Adams, Henry, 98
After-life, 100
Aglaia, 16
agricultural mythology, 44
Annunciation, 90
apocalypse, 106–7
Apollo, 16
Aristotle, 34
art, 96
Arthur, King, 30
ass, 66
astrology, 44, 61
"atheists," 48

atonement, 22, 91. *See also* re-
    demption

B

battle, mysticism of, 91
Bible: central myth, 57; legends,
    54–55. *See also* Old Testament;
    specific topics
Biblical myths, xii–xiv, 3, 25, 47.
    See also Judeo-Christian
    tradition
birds, 78
Black Madonna, 97
blame, 112
Brahman, 47
Buber, Martin, 60, 107
Buddha (Siddartha Gautama), 26,
    51, 61–63, 68–69, 71–72, 75;
    infant deeds, 68

Buddhism, 20, 51
bull, 89

C

Campbell, Joseph: bibliography,
    121–22; end of his life, xvi; life
    of mythic hero, 102–3;
    misinterpretations of and false
    statements about, xii,
    xvi–xvii; religious
    heritage, xv, 59; writings,
    vii, 102
caste system, 5, 59
Catholicism, xv, xvi, 33, 59. *See
    also* Mass
cause, secret, 34–35
cave, motif of birth in a, 65–66
Celts, 40
ceremonial rituals, 93–94
Cakras, 99
Chartres, 96–98
child: as teacher, 68–70. *See also*
    infant
Christ: of the Second Coming, 97.
    See also Jesus Christ; *specific
    topics*
Christianity, 61. *See also* Judeo-
    Christian tradition; *specific
    topics*
clergy, 33
compassion, x, xi, xvii–xviii, 21,
    22, 99
consciousness: identification
    with, 20–21; reconciling it
    to the preconditions of its
    existence, 2–3

Copernicus, 105
Corpus hermeticum, 37, 38
Creator, 27, 43–44, 53, 90.
    See also God
credo, 62
Cross, 35, 76–83. *See also*
    crucifixion
crucifixion, xvi, 22, 58, 66,
    76, 77, 82, 111–12;
    reason for Jesus's, 27.
    See also Cross

D

death, 34–35; life after, 100
Devil, 22, 76, 77, 87–88
devils, 41
dharma, 64
dissociation, mythic, 5, 12

E

Earth, 105–6
Easter, 103–5, 107, 111–13
Eckhart, Meister, 29, 110
ego, 100
Egypt, flight into, 68
emotions, tragic, 34
End of the World, xviii,
    19, 83
Essene community, 70
eternity, 89–90
ethical *vs.* mystical religious
    perspectives, 16
ethnicity, 107–8
evil. *See* good and evil
exile, 57

F

faith, 13
Fall (Garden of Eden), 14–16, 22,
    23, 41, 51–52
fear, 34; *vs.* desire, 51
fertility rites, 14
Fight into Egypt, 68
Flood: mythologies in the story of
    the, 43
Freud, Sigmund, 86
fruit of the knowledge of good
    and evil, 50

G

Garden of Eden, 14–16, 50. *See
    also* Genesis; Tree(s)
gender. *See* male and female
Genesis, 4, 45, 49–53
Gnostic Gospel of Thomas, 19–20
Gnosticism, 48, 58
God, 11–13, 39; as an It, 44, 52;
    elements of human
    experience of the mystery
    of, 24–28; identification
    with, 19; as metaphor, 19;
    notions of, 17–20, 60; as
    symbol, 48
Goddess, 41–42, 47–49, 93
gods, 18; kinds of, 43–49
good and evil, 16, 50
Goodall, Jane, 21–22
Gottfried von Strassburg, 90
Graces, 16
Grail, 88, 89
Grail King, 23
Greek ritual world, 94

H

Hallaj, 27
heart: awakening the, 33
Heaven, 20, 97
Hell, 81, 100
Hero with a Thousand Faces, The
    (Campbell), 102
heroes: on a spiritual journey,
    ordinary people as, 88–89.
    See also savior-hero
Hero's Journey, 87
Hinduism, 58–59, 64, 82
Hitler, Adolf, 95
Holy Land, 36
Horus, 66

I

"I-Thou" *vs.* "I-It" relationships, 107
identification, 58; with conscious-
    ness, 20–21; with God, 19
identity, 26
imagination: active, 38, 39; and
    theological inquiry, 37–42
India, 5. *See also specific topics*
infant/infancy story, 66–68
initiation ceremonies, 93–94
Inner Reaches of Outer Space, The, 20
interpretive function of mythol-
    ogy, 3–4
intuition, 81
Islam, 61–62

J

Jacob and Esau, 55
Jainism, 46

Jesus Christ, 19; birth and horo-
     scope, 61 (*see also* infant;
     Virgin Birth); and laws,
     87–88; and love, 87, 88, 90; as
     Messiah, 70–72; original
     Christians' understanding of,
     87; resurrection and ascen-
     dance to Heaven, 19, 20, 48;
     as teacher, 68. *See also specific
     topics*
John the Baptist, 69–71
Joseph Campbell Foundation, vii
Joseph (Old Testament), 55–56
Joyce, James, 34, 63
Judaism, 55, 57, 58, 68, 69; as
     religion of participation *vs.*
     identification, 58. *See also
     specific topics*
Judas, 75
Judeo-Christian tradition, xi–xiv,
     xviii–xix, 27–28; Hero's
     Journey and, 87–88. *See also
     specific topics*
judgment, 50
Jung, Carl Gustav, 13, 38, 60,
     79–82, 106, 108

K

Kansa, King, 67
Kant, Immanuel, 17, 47
karma, cyclic, 43
Kennedy, Eugene, vii–viii
King, Martin Luther, Jr., 35
Kingdom of Heaven, 20
Kingdom of the Father, 19, 51

Kṛṣṇa, 67
Kuṇḍalini, 98

L

Last Supper, 73–75
law(s), 87–88; redemption from
     curse of the, 87
legends, 54
life after death, 100
life stages and crises: mythology as
     carrying people through, 5
light and illumination, 20–21, 72,
     75. *See also* Mithra
love, 87, 88, 90; and marriage, 92

M

Magi, 65
male and female, 42, 52, 53, 82, 93.
     See also Goddess
Mandala symbolism, 80
Mann, Thomas, 55
marriage, 23, 25, 91–92
Mary, Mother of Jesus, 20, 42, 97.
     See also Virgin Birth
Mass, 88, 95
mathematics, 4
Maya, 17, 63
Mayans, 78
meditation, 16; discursive and
     ordered, 14
menstruation, 93, 94
Mesopotamian people, 49
Messiah, 70–72. *See also* Christ;
     Jesus Christ
metaphor(s), 34; of Bible, 4; as

facts, 48; misunderstood, 48; and mystery, 8–9; as native tongue of myth, 6–8; origin of word, xiv; religious mystery, myth, and, 48

Miracles, 72–73

Mithra, 65–66

moon, 89, 90, 105, 113

moral order, mythologies validating and supporting, 5

Moses, 37, 56, 74, 87

Mother Universe, 97

mystery: experiencing, 12–16; symbolism and religious, 11–12. *See also* under metaphor(s)

mysticism, 109

mythic dissociation, 5, 12

mythological images, 86

mythologies: fragmented, 86–87; nature and antinature, 41, 47; primitive, 3

mythology: definition and nature of, x, xii, 111; in our time, problem of, 86; purpose, 12–13; and remythologization, 111

myth(s): functions, 2–5, 103; meaning, 1–2, 102; metaphor as the native tongue of, 6–8; origin, 23, 24

N

nature, 41, 47

Navaho, 36

O

Oedipus, 36

Old Testament, 41, 47, 58, 86; Christianity and, 57. *See also* Biblical myths; *specific topics*

Orient, 27, 28, 59, 88, 90

Osiris, 66

Othin, 79

P

Passover, 95, 103–5, 107, 112, 113

Patriarchs, 54, 55

Paul, St., 22, 39, 57–58, 81–82, 87

Peay, Pythia, xvi

Peter, St., 75

Pharoah, 56

pigs/boars, 75

pity, 34

Plato, 52

Promised Land, 7, 36

psychological functions, four basic, 80–82

Purgatory, 100

Q

Queste del Saint Graal, 30

R

Rank, Otto, 56

rebirth, 89–90

redemption, 23–24, 76, 87. *See also* atonement

reincarnation, 100

relationships, 21, 23, 91, 107. *See also* marriage
religions: interpreting symbols historically, 86, 109–10; leaders of institutional, xv; as protecting against religious experience, 13–14, 18, 60; three world, 61–62; Western, 11–12, 27
religious belief, 62
religious function of mythology, 12–13
religious perspectives, ethical *vs.* mystical, 16
resurrection. *See* Easter
rites of passage, 93–94
ritual, 92–95; dangers, 95; individual participation in, 94–95

S

sacred space, 95–96
salvation, 75
Satan. *See* Devil
savior-hero, 62, 71, 72, 78, 82. *See also specific individuals*
Schopenhauer, Arthur, ix–x, 91
Schrödinger, Erwin, 13
science, 4
Second Coming of Christ, 97
Seder meal at Passover, 95
separation and union, 53
serpent, 75, 89
Set, 65–66
shadow, 75
sin, 12, 100

Space Age, 103–5, 107–9
suffering, ix, xi, 34
Sumero-Babylonian complex, 25
sun, 89, 105
symbols, 6, 25, 102; mythological, 8; as out of place and time, 28–31; psychoanalytic interpretation of, 86; religions' historical interpretation of, 86, 109–10; religious, 34, 109. *See also specific symbols*

T

Temptations, 71–72, 88
terror, 34
"Thou art that" *(Tat tvam asi)*, ix, x, xi, xviii, xix, 13, 20, 26
time and space, 17
Tower of Babel, 54
tragic emotions, 34
transcendence, 13, 16, 18, 39, 47–48, 87, 91, 95; how to achieve, 92–94; meaning and nature of, 92
Tree(s), 14–15, 50–51, 78–80
2001: A Space Odyssey, 108

U

UFOs, 108
union, separation and, 53

V

Vasu, 64
Virgin, 98

Virgin Birth, 7, 20, 29, 62–65, 90,
  106. *See also* infant
Vyasa, 63–65

W

Waste Land, 23
water, 74
Western tradition, 11–12, 27, 28,
  31 world of the general and
  the individual, 21

Y

Yggdrasil, 79–80
yoga, Kuṇḍalinī, 98

Z

Zen Buddhism, 20
Zodiac, signs of, 44, 61
Zoroaster, 3, 46
Zoroastrianism/Zoroastrian
  religion, 3, 46–47

ABOUT THE AUTHOR

JOSEPH CAMPBELL was an American author and teacher best known for his work in the field of comparative mythology. He was born in New York City in 1904, and from early childhood he became interested in mythology. He loved to read books about American Indian cultures, and frequently visited the American Museum of Natural History in New York, where he was fascinated by the museum's collection of totem poles. Campbell was educated at Columbia University, where he specialized in medieval literature and, after earning a master's degree, continued his studies at universities in Paris and Munich. While abroad he was influenced by the art of Pablo Picasso and Henri Matisse, the novels of James Joyce and Thomas Mann, and the psychological studies of Sigmund Freud and Carl Jung. These encounters led to Campbell's theory that all myths and epics are linked in the human psyche, and that they are cultural manifestations of the universal need to explain social, cosmological, and spiritual realities.

After a period in California, where he encountered John Steinbeck and the biologist Ed Ricketts, he taught at the Canterbury School, and then, in 1934, joined the literature department at Sarah Lawrence College, a post he retained for many years. During the 1940s and '50s, he helped Swami

Nikhilananda to translate the *Upanishads* and *The Gospel of Sri Ramakrishna.* He also edited works by the German scholar Heinrich Zimmer on Indian art, myths, and philosophy. In 1944, with Henry Morton Robinson, Campbell published *A Skeleton Key to Finnegans Wake.* His first original work, *The Hero with a Thousand Faces,* came out in 1949 and was immediately well received; in time, it became acclaimed as a classic. In this study of the "myth of the hero," Campbell asserted that there is a single pattern of heroic journey and that all cultures share this essential pattern in their various heroic myths. In his book he also outlined the basic conditions, stages, and results of the archetypal hero's journey.

Joseph Campbell died in 1987. In 1988, a series of television interviews with Bill Moyers, *The Power of Myth,* introduced Campbell's views to millions of people.

ABOUT THE
JOSEPH CAMPBELL FOUNDATION

THE JOSEPH CAMPBELL FOUNDATION (JCF) is a nonprofit corporation that continues the work of Joseph Campbell, exploring the fields of mythology and comparative religion. The Foundation is guided by three principal goals:

First, the Foundation preserves, protects, and perpetuates Campbell's pioneering work. This includes cataloging and archiving his works, developing new publications based on his works, directing the sale and distribution of his published works, protecting copyrights to his works, and increasing awareness of his works by making them available in digital formats on JCF's Web site.

Second, the Foundation promotes the study of mythology and comparative religion. This involves implementing and/or supporting diverse mythological education programs, supporting and/or sponsoring events designed to increase public awareness, donating Campbell's archived works (principally to the Joseph Campbell and Marija Gimbutas Archive and Library), and utilizing JCF's Web site as a forum for relevant cross-cultural dialogue.

Third, the Foundation helps individuals enrich their lives by participating in a series of programs, including our global, Internet-based Associates program, our local international network of Mythological Roundtables, and our periodic Joseph Campbell related events and activities.

For more information on Joseph Campbell
and the Joseph Campbell Foundation, contact:

JOSEPH CAMPBELL FOUNDATION
www.jcf.org
Post Office Box 36
San Anselmo, CA 94979-0036
E-mail: info@jcf.org